THE

Language

OF A

DISTANT SHORE

(দূরবর্তী তটের ভাষা)

Rezwana Chowdhury

ISBN

Hardcover: 979-8-90190-140-3

Paperback: 979-8-90190-139-7

About the Author

Rezwana Chowdhury is a Bengali American author who immigrated to the United States at the age of twelve. After earning degrees from the City University of New York and DePaul University, she discovered her true calling in healthcare and is now completing her Doctor of Nursing Practice (DNP).

Guided by her love of history, philosophy, and the quiet wisdom of nature, Rezwana writes about the strength and beauty found in everyday lives. The Language of a Distant Shore is dedicated to the healthcare professionals who serve tirelessly with compassion and courage, with selfless intent to help others.

Her greatest inspiration and joy come from her children, her most genuine gems. Her anchors are her friends and family.

Prelude

The story you're about to encounter was born during my time on the Covid Unit, stemming from quiet nights alone with grief and reflection. During that unprecedented time, I learned what truly matters: the hearts we touch, the memories we cherish, and the ability to gently let go.

To my son and daughter—you are my steady light, my rock, my joy. You are, without question, two of the most extraordinary souls I have ever known. To my parents and family, thank you for giving all you could to help me stand where I am today. To the friends who have stayed close to my heart—your presence has been a quiet blessing, and your love is an anchor.

Table of Contents

About The Author i

Prelude...ii

Florida June 2019 1

  The Power Of Moonlight 1

Khulna, Bangladesh 1978-1980 4

  The Beginning In The White Bungalow 4

  Sudden Sense Of Acceptance And Let Go.............................6

  Curious Kalapuri 8

Florida 11

  The Edges Of Memory 11

Florida March 2020 18

  Garden Of The Mind 18

Dhaka, Bangladesh 1982-1984: 21

  Kalapuri's Window Seat...21

  Kalapuri's Air Diary 23

  Kalapuri's Invisible Pen...25

  Pickles And Petals 26

  Dancing Fish And Mystic Pond 28

  The Ripples Of Fate...31

  The Fish..33

  Back To Dhaka And Back To School...................................35

Florida July 2020 38

  Fragments Of Memories 38

The New Horizon..44

  Dhaka, 1990 44

  Alta Loma, California, 1990...44

Los Angeles, California 1991-1992 48

    Unbroken 48

Florida January 2021...54

    The Last Plea 54

    Core Humanism 58

    Presence 61

NYC High School 1993- 1996 66

    Unspoken 66

Florida Sept 2021..71

    The Enigma Of Belonging 71

British India 1910...74

    The Forest Of Betrayal...74

British India...77

    The Uninvited Union 77

Florida September 2021 82

    Flux 82

    Whispers From A Distant Shore.................................83

    Deliverance 88

    British India 1910..89

    Florida 2021 91

Florida June 2019

The Power Of Moonlight

It was night under a full moon. A lifeless, unclothed body lay flat on the ground, hair neatly draped over one shoulder, hands by the sides, and toes pointing outward. Upon closer inspection, she realized it was herself in the grave. The body was decomposed, with skin appearing bright blue and gray, lacking all muscular tone, and covered in dirt. As she approached to examine it further, she saw critters, including cockroaches and worms, on her face…and the corpse opened her eye…

She jumped out of her nightmare, barely catching her breath, and sweating. She had trouble sleeping all night, and when she finally did, she had this nightmare. She never dreams, never! This was one of the first nightmares she's had since she was little.

It was a summer morning, and when she looked at her clock, it was 4 am. She was sleepless in the predawn darkness, tossing and turning, unable to go back to sleep. She got up and decided to watch the sunrise at the beach. Her two kids were sleeping, the 12-year-old daughter was with her, and the 16-year-old son was sleeping in a different bedroom. Without trying to make any noise, she went to her closet and got dressed. She left a note on the table for the kids, but she often goes to the beach.

It was pitch dark, but the crescent moon was shaped, and the stars lit her way. She took a few moments to look at the moon, and a soft smile appeared on the corner of her lips.

She lived 10 miles from the beach, and the roads were empty. As she approached the beach, the police officer was opening the gate.

The officer showed his hand, and she slowly rolled her window down to hear him say, "Ma'am, it sure is early to come to the beach." The officer paused to look at his watch and said, "At 5:32 am, stay safe."

She nodded and said, "Thank you." She parked her car and noticed the moon was still on her right side, beaming ever so brightly. In the midst of darkness, the moon seemed much brighter and closer. She always loved the moon and the stars. She is, in fact, fascinated by them and has even named them.

Her favorite star is the one that accompanies the moon. When the moon is crescent-shaped, that star seems to be talking to the moon and sitting at a 30-degree angle from the base of the moon. She named that star serendipity. Just like the meaning, the star is her anchor in life; that star comforted her year after year, when no person could. She always finds extreme strength through the stars.

As she walked towards the beach, she felt nostalgic; she was in a different time, and perhaps in a different space. She thought of how the beauty of the sky never gets old, fades, or becomes boring. Every time, it brings her the utmost joy. She finds a spot to sit and closes her eyes, her face slightly upward to the sky. Her legs are close to her chest, slightly supporting her hands as she puts her toes on the sand. She felt profound happiness, thinking that when she is in nature, she is herself, no judgments, no preconceived ideas, no society, no religious bigotry. She is one with the sand, sky, and ocean. She feels in the moment of awe.

She wondered if maybe we all need to experience this moment where we fall out of time and space, where the body feels like it's moving, and the mind is full of gratitude. Perhaps this is the time she is truly herself. As the sun starts to come up, you notice that she is thin, has brown skin, and black curly hair. Her name is Nilima.

She opened her eyes and felt a great sense of contentment within her. She is always drawn to the ocean, as if it is calling her to come and feel the cold water on her feet. She also feels extreme fear of the water, its ferocity, tenacity, and ability to consume worries her.

As the sunlight spilled over the horizon, touching the sand and the tips of the waves, Nilima's mind seemed to unravel time itself. The fragmented piece of her life flashed before her eyes, not as memories stored in fragments but as vivid, unfolding scenes she could almost step into: the quiet bungalow in Khulna, the scent of rain on earth, the laughter and cries of childhood, the small discoveries of ants and butterflies, and the whispered songs of her grandmother.

Every sensation was immediate—the grit of sand beneath her toes, the faint salt on her lips from the ocean breeze, the warmth of the sun spreading across her skin. For the first time, she experienced a state of being that was completely present: every sight, sound, and emotion coexisting in perfect clarity. It was as if the universe had compressed itself into a single, infinite moment, and she was both observer and participant, fully awake and yet suspended in the timelessness of awe.

Khulna, Bangladesh 1978-1980

The Beginning In The White Bungalow

She saw herself when she was born, as if she were observing and not physically there. She was in Khulna, the southwest part of Bangladesh. Her mother was in labor, and it was in a house full of women, who were surrounding her. She stepped out of the room and saw that she was in a white bungalow. The one that her mother always talked about.

This bungalow was situated far from the city. It was gated, and as you entered through the gate, it had a long driveway surrounded by trees and many different flower plants. The bungalow had a wrap-around veranda. Mother loved living in the Khulna bungalow, Nilima remembered her mother talking about the cook who loved her very much. Always helping her with not just cooking, but he was some sort of mentor, guiding her to understand life. Nilima decided to see if she could find the cook.

She headed straight to the kitchen through the outdoor corridor. She saw many plants, including pots with various kinds of flowers and evergreen plants. She felt at ease, and an extremely familiar vibe rushed through her body. She used to run through these corridors many times. She looked at the sky; it must be dawn, with November fog surrounding the whole house. It was November 5th, and she had realized it would be Sunday. She remembered her mother always telling her, "You are born on a Sunday. Sunday babies are usually stubborn." Those words echoed as she walked towards the kitchen.

As she approached the kitchen, she saw these middle-aged men making tea and sitting on a stool. He was making tea for at least 10 people; the teacups were arranged on a serving tray. As he meticulously poured the tea into the cups, he was singing. A very familiar song, Nilima recognizes the song being played many times; perhaps she heard it while growing up in NYC. In fact, she remembers the song very well; it was one of her father's favorite songs.

Sokhi, bhaabona kaahare bole.

Sokhi, jaatona kaahare bole.

Tomra je balo dibaso-rajanee bhaalobasa bhaalobasa -

Sokhi, bhaalobasa kaare koy!

Se ki keboli jatonamoy.

Se ki keboli chokher jal? Se ki keboli dukher shwas?

Loke tabe kare ki sukheri tare emon dukher aash…

(What do you mean by 'Thought,' my dear.

What do you mean by 'Pain' either.

What is that you yell 'Love' for,

What the word 'Love' means,

Is it saturated with pain?

Is that synonymous with tears or a sigh of suffering?

It is surely a wonder why it fascinates people.)

She started singing with him and caught herself off guard when she realized he could neither be seen nor heard. She stopped singing and followed him as he carried all the teacups carefully, not to spill a single drop of tea.

He took the tray to the room where my father and grandfather were sitting. They weren't talking to each other, just awkwardly sitting across from each other, pretending they were busy with their own thoughts. Father was reading a newspaper, wearing traditional Bengali clothes. Grandfather stood up rather awkwardly and started sipping tea and pacing in the room.

Nilima now approached the room she initially found herself in. Nilima thought she saw her grandmother at the bedside, waiting for me.

Suddenly, someone called out, "Aibar chele na hole moina mia onak rege jabe," (if it's not a boy this time, the grandfather will not be happy). Indeed, she was born. She is dark skinned and has brown hair, Nilima. Someone said, "onak kalo holo maye ta" (she is pretty dark). The whole room was quiet as she took her first breath and cried.

She was the 5th girl in the Chowdhury family; she has three cousins and one sister. The grandmother was beaming with joy and saying "shusto bacca, haat paa shob ache" (healthy baby, she has all fingers and toes). The grandmother repeated the exact words several times as if she were chanting. There was a knock on the door, and the men wanted to know if the child was a boy or a girl. The grandmother came out of the room and showed the baby.

The grandfather didn't look at her when he learned that the child was a girl, and he walked out of the house. The grandmother was disappointed and shouted, It's a healthy child!

Sudden Sense Of Acceptance And Let Go

A few months passed when Nilima started to crawl. She would sit at her grandfather's feet and look up at him. One day, the grandfather was sitting on the Veranda sipping tea and reading a newspaper.

Suddenly, he heard "ooga aaga" and found Nilima at his feet, looking up to him and smiling. The grandfather stopped reading and called her mother to get Nilima. After a few instances, her grandfather picked her up one day and held her facing him. Nilima rested both her hands on his cheeks and her lips on his nose.

At that moment, as Nilima rested her small hands against his cheeks and pressed her lips gently to his nose, the grandfather felt an unexpected warmth surge through him. A wave of acceptance and unconditional love seemed to fill the Veranda. The little girl, so tiny and yet so fearless in her affection, had broken through the walls he had built around his heart over the years. From that instant, a quiet bond was forged, and gradually, as days turned into months, Nilima became his favorite. His constant companion in moments of solitude, his source of amusement, and the child whose laughter could brighten the heaviness of his routine.

Nilima was far from what anyone would call delicate or fragile in appearance. She wasn't the fairest among the children of the Chowdhury family; her skin was dark, her curls were untamed, and her movements often bold and untethered. Yet, it was precisely her spirited nature, her curiosity, and her warmth that made her utterly lovable. She had a way of observing the world with wide-eyed intensity, asking questions without needing answers, and of drawing others into the quiet wonder she carried within her.

Her grandmother, in contrast, fell in love at first sight. From the moment she held Nilima in her arms, she saw something familiar, an echo of herself in the child's dark skin. The rich curls that framed her face, and the curious, peapod-shaped eyes that seemed to soak in every detail around her.

There was an almost uncanny resemblance that delighted her grandmother, and she lavished Nilima with care, play, and tender guidance. She taught her little games, showed her how to navigate the household world, and offered comfort in ways only a grandmother could.

Yet, life, as it often does, did not remain static. Seasons changed, people grew older, circumstances shifted, and the rhythms of the household transformed with time. Joy and love persisted, but they were inevitably mingled with loss, responsibility, and the subtle changes that mark the passage of life. Still, amid these shifts, the bond Nilima shared with her grandfather and grandmother left an indelible mark on her heart, a foundation of warmth, acceptance, and the first lessons of what it means to be cherished.

Grandmother recently became very sick; Nilima crawled her way to her grandmother's room every morning, trying to get into bed. Nilima thought, "Why does my playing friend not want to play anymore?" Why is she always sleeping? Unable to understand, she would fuss and force her grandmother to go into the veranda. In fact, when she was 13 months old, her grandmother died. Nilima's clothes were found under her pillow. They said the grandmother would often smell the sweet fragrance of Nilima, now that she was bedridden. For a few days after her death, Nilima came to her room regularly but could not find her, then she would look for her outside.

Nilima wondered, her small heart heavy with a confusion she could not yet name: Where is she? Where is the gentle presence with glasses who lifted me from the floor every morning and carried me outside into the soft dawn light? Where is the one who offered me food, placing biscuits carefully in my tiny hands, as if nourishing not just my body, but something unseen within me? These questions lingered in the quiet corners of her mind, unanswered yet resonating with a deeper awareness she could not articulate.

For a while, she searched endlessly, crawling to the familiar room each morning, hoping to find the warmth and comfort that had become a part of her rhythm. But gradually, the absence became a presence of its own, a silent teacher whispering that life moves, that love transforms, and that the soul must begin its own journey of discovery.

Finally, Nilima stopped crawling to that room. She turned her attention outward, drawn irresistibly to the world beyond the walls of the bungalow. The garden, the earth, the whisper of leaves in the breeze, the intricate colonies of ants, and the flight of butterflies—all seemed to call to her in a voice older and wiser than any humans. It was as if the universe itself was extending a hand, inviting her to witness the sacred dance of life in all its minutiae.

In the quiet of those early explorations, Nilima sensed something profound: that the love she had known was not lost, only transformed, flowing through the earth, the air, and the living creatures around her. Each step on the soft soil, each gaze at a fluttering butterfly, each careful observation of the ant's tunnels felt like a communion, a sacred dialogue with existence itself. She began to understand, in the pure, unfiltered way of a child, that absence and presence are intertwined, that loss can open the heart to wonder, and that life is fragile, fleeting, and infinitely intricate. It offers its mysteries to those willing to see.

And so, she wandered further, not in sorrow, but in awe, discovering that the world outside was a mirror of something deeper within. A universe alive with lessons, love, and quiet revelations waiting to be embraced…

Curious Kalapuri

When Nilima began to walk, she quickly became her grandfather's most cherished companion. Everyone affectionately called her Kalapuri, the dark girl. Recognizing not only her skin tone but the brightness of her spirit that seemed to illuminate every space she entered. The Chowdhury household had shifted after her grandmother's passing: her older aunt had moved away with her children, seeking a new life with her husband, while the younger aunt, barely twelve herself, remained at home. Her grandfather returned to his village, leaving Nilima's father frequently away on highway projects as the lead engineer, and her mother shouldering almost all domestic responsibilities.

Yet Nilima thrived in this transformed household. The outdoors became her sanctuary. She was endlessly fascinated by the tiny worlds she discovered, including colonies of fire ants and carpenter ants, their intricate tunnels, and the communal cooperation that captivated her young mind. She would crouch beside the sand, careful not to disturb their work, marveling at how they carried objects twice their size, and how they shared their labor across countless tiny bodies. During the rainy season, she would check on the colonies after the downpour, inspecting damage and recovery, her eyes wide with wonder.

Her explorations often left her toes and legs riddled with ant bites, but Nilima never cried. Pain was a mere detail; her curiosity was far larger. Leaves and sticks became treasures, collected and hidden in secret places, each one a piece of her growing world.

Her mother, exhausted from pregnancy and the constant demands of household life, often fretted over Nilima's wandering spirit, "Ishhh Ai maye ta k neye ar parlam na, akta kotha shune na," (I can't deal with this girl; she never listens.) She would sigh, frustrated that the child never seemed to obey. One afternoon, panic overtook her when Nilima was found on the driveway, her knee bleeding after trying to pry the bumper off an old car with a stick. The child had not cried, merely observed the injury as if studying it. Taken to the hospital, Nilima's bed faced a window where sunlight streamed onto a garden alive with bees. Even there, she noticed which flowers the honeybees preferred, her mind cataloging every detail.

Once home, Nilima returned to her routine of quiet observation. Water flowing after rain, the underground breathing of ants, and the family dynamics of tiny creatures, all these became puzzles she examined endlessly, though she never spoke the questions aloud. Her fascination with crawling, scuttling, and flying creatures grew, forming the foundation of a lifelong attentiveness to the living world.

One afternoon, as her mother rested in a rare moment of exhaustion, Nilima escaped once more. She wandered into a fragrant garden where butterflies danced above blossoms in a riot of color. Following a particularly vibrant butterfly, she settled onto the soft earth, legs crossed, her eyes fixed on the delicate creature. Absorbed in observation, she leaned back, unaware of the dangers around her.

A cobra, coiled and silent, slithered nearby. Nilima froze, a calm awareness washing over her, sensing no immediate threat. The snake moved closer, yet she remained still, understanding without words that she was part of the same living world, subject to its rhythms but not yet its cruelty. When the butterfly finally left, she rose carefully, one inch from the serpent, and followed its path until it settled. She noticed it resting, unusually still, and gently placed a leaf over it, as if acknowledging its vulnerability.

Nilima's mother eventually found her, sleeping beside the now lifeless butterfly, and carried her inside. Though exasperated by her daughter's disobedience, Nilima's mother marveled at her resilience and independence. Nilima's spirited nature, her singing, her persistence, and her refusal to complain about discomfort were framed as the "Sunday child," stubbornness, which her mother often repeated to console herself. The pediatrician assured her that Nilima was growing perfectly, hitting every developmental milestone with exceptional cognitive and physical growth.

Yet for Nilima, development wasn't measured in milestones. It was measured in wonder, in the silent communion with nature, and in the questions she held in her mind but never voiced. She did not yet understand the impermanence of presence—why people leave, why lives change. Still, she was learning the delicate art of observation, of curiosity, and of finding connection in every corner of the world around her. In these early days, Nilima was learning the rhythm of life itself, one tiny, miraculous moment at a time.

Florida

The Edges Of Memory

Nilima suddenly felt a warm touch on her hand. She looked up, and it was a dog. The owner said, "I am sorry." She shook her head and said, "It's ok, you have a cute dog." Sunrise was complete, and she felt awkward in her own skin, unable to realize how that had happened, why the memories felt so alive. What she just saw could not be her memories; these stories were told to her over the years, but no one has ever described them in this vivid and elaborate way.

She could not deduce how she knew the most minor details, like how the ant's tunnel looked, or how she observed her injury, or even where she would save the sticks. She pondered, "No one has told her the information that no one witnessed but herself, and I could not have possibly remembered in such great detail."

She knows that memories don't start to form until the age of 3. When kids get older, memories lose their content until 7 years of age, that's when we start constructing concrete memories. Why did it feel so real? How am I able to travel to the past and yet feel it happen now? However, her present moment is in Florida, 4 feet away from the Atlantic Ocean, with the sun rays on her skin, and her long curly hair is gently dancing with the wind. For whatever reason, she felt she was in a different place at the same time. She continued to wonder, we never really know when time started, and it is truly a prediction.

Time is eternal and dynamic, she thought, because what she felt disproves everything; she thought she knew about time, that we have past, present, and future. However, she argued to herself, time is the most elusive thing because once you have a memory of something, it is also part of the present; it is always part of you.

This experience today made her wonder what can be voluntarily remembered? Why was the state of herself shifted to a place she didn't think about? She wanted to continue remembering what had happened in her past. This must be a sign, she thought.

She came home and found the kids still sleeping. She took a shower and kept thinking about what had happened at the beach today. She pinched herself to see if she was here, now today. She screamed, "Ouch," and thought, "I must be going crazy." She could not understand why she could remember details from her past, "My God…I was being born! How could I have had such deep thoughts about things around me and never have had any memory of them? Is it possible? Did it ever happen to someone else? Is my deep-rooted consciousness trying to tell me something? I need to answer," she thought. As she was making breakfast for the kids, she hesitated if she should even tell the kids what she experienced. Her children usually laugh at her obsession with nature walks and taking pictures of leaves, bees, and butterflies. She decided not to say anything to them. Her search for answers began at the library, where she read various psychological articles about human memory.

All she found was that scientists, psychologists, and researchers seemed to arrive at similar conclusions—human memories are indeed formed in the early years. Still, true access to them does not begin until around the age of six or seven. Research in developmental psychology calls this childhood amnesia, the strange forgetting of the first years of life.

Carole Peterson, a researcher at Canada's Memorial University of Newfoundland, had shown that children as young as two may form explicit memories, the kind tied to facts or stories we can later tell. But these fragile imprints fade, overwritten by time. The deeper implicit memories, the sensory impressions, the body's way of remembering, emerge only around the age of seven, when the brain's hippocampus matures enough to bind moments into narrative. Before then, experience exists, but it floats in fragments.

Yet science could not explain the way Nilima had traveled. She had not simply recalled. She had been there, entire, vivid, inhabiting the past while standing in the present.

Nilima leaned back in her chair, the blue glow of her laptop screen staining the walls of her room. The articles she had spent hours reading began to blur, but one name kept surfacing again and again: Carole Peterson.

Peterson was a child psychologist who had spent decades studying how memories formed, endured, and, most importantly, disappeared. Nilima found herself captivated, as if the research spoke directly to her own restless longing. According to Peterson, children as young as two could form explicit memories, those snapshots of events tied to facts and stories. But by the time they reached adulthood, many of these recollections vanished into silence, swept under the tide of what scientists called childhood amnesia.

Nilima frowned, scrolling. That phrase, childhood amnesia, felt heavy, clinical, but it matched her own experience of the void she carried. So much of her early life had been erased, and yet she was certain something remained, hidden just beyond reach.

Peterson's studies suggested that memory was not as fixed as people assumed. Children often remember vividly in their early years, but by the age of ten, even those memories slip away. And when they did resurface later, people tended to postdate them, placing themselves older than they actually were in the memory. Nilima whispered the word aloud: telescoping. As though the past itself bent and stretched, forever retreating from touch.

Yet what struck her most was not the science of forgetting, but the fragile exceptions that Peterson uncovered. Some memories, she found, endured for decades unchanged, unshaken, anchored by emotion, by the intensity of the bond between child and parent.

Peterson even discovered that children who shared deeper emotional ties with their mothers could access more of these early memories, while closeness to fathers seemed linked to recalling the earliest memories of all.

Nilima thought of her own mother, bustling in the kitchen on school mornings, coaxing her with endearments: "Amar shona Kala Puri… Ma sotti." The words came back with a clarity that startled her. Was this a memory she had carried all along? Or was she reconstructing it, piecing fragments together with what she wished had endured?

As she closed her eyes, Peterson's voice lingered through the research papers: Memory is not fixed; it is shaped by time, by questions, by the way we search for it. Nilima realized with a jolt that her obsession might be the very thing reshaping what she found. Perhaps that was why her vision at the beach had felt so vivid; it had bypassed recall entirely. She hadn't remembered; she had been there.

And if memory could bend that way beyond the brain, beyond childhood amnesia, then what else could it hold? Could it stretch not only backward into her early years, but further still, into lives lived before?

Nilima exhaled slowly, the screen now dark before her. Science had given her a map of forgetting, but it also left her with an even more urgent question: if memories could be lost, reshaped, or telescoped into later years, then what exactly had she touched at the beach?

Not a memory, surely. Something else. Something older.

She pressed her palms together, as though in prayer, whispering to herself in the quiet room: There has to be more.

Was it memory? Or something else entirely?

Neuroscientists spoke of synaptic pruning, where neural pathways have trimmed and reshaped themselves in childhood, wiping away early recollections. But mystics spoke differently; they suggested that what is lost to the mind may remain in the consciousness, imprinted beyond the folds of the brain. Some traditions described it as the akashic records—a vast archive of human experience, past and present, accessible only when the veil of ordinary awareness becomes thin.

The concept was both fascinating and perplexing. Synaptic pruning was the process by which the brain eliminates excess synapses— connections between neurons—that are no longer needed. This process, she learned, was crucial for the efficient functioning of the brain, allowing it to strengthen the most used connections and discard the rest.

As she delved deeper into her research, Nilima discovered that the phenomenon of synaptic pruning was first identified in the 1970s by Peter Huttenlocher, a pediatric neurologist and neuroscientist at the University of Chicago.

Huttenlocher's groundbreaking work involved examining the brains of infants and young children, revealing that synapses are overproduced during early development and then pruned back as the brain matures.

This discovery was revolutionary. It challenged the prevailing belief that the brain's structure was static after a certain age. Instead, Huttenlocher's research demonstrated that the brain was dynamic, continuously reshaping itself in response to experience.

Nilima pondered the implications of this. If the brain could reshape itself, could memories be reshaped too? Could her own memories, some of which felt so distant and fragmented, be reconnected or even altered?

Her thoughts were interrupted by a soft knock on the door. It was her son, holding a tray with a cup of tea and a plate of biscuits.

"Thought you might need a break," the son said with a smile.

"Thanks, pumpkin," Nilima replied, accepting the tea. As she took a sip, she felt a warmth spread through her, a comfort that contrasted with the swirling questions in her mind.

"You're still thinking about the past, aren't you?" son asked, sitting beside her.

Nilima nodded. "I just... I want to understand. I want to remember more."

Her son placed a gentle hand on her shoulder, "Sometimes, it's not about remembering everything. It's about accepting what we have and finding peace with it."

Nilima thought, "Wow, my son is so much wiser than I thought."

Nilima looked at her son, seeing the wisdom in his eyes. Perhaps, she thought, the key wasn't in trying to force the past into her present but in allowing herself to live fully in the now.

As she resumed her research, Nilima found herself reflecting on the concept of synaptic pruning—not just as a biological process but as a metaphor for her own journey. Just as the brain discards unused synapses to make way for stronger connections, perhaps she, too, needed to let go of old, unhelpful memories to make space for new experiences and growth.

In this light, her quest to understand the past became not just an intellectual pursuit but a path to personal healing. The garden of her mind, she realized, could be cultivated, pruned, and nurtured, allowing her to flourish in ways she had never imagined.

Nilima lingered on that thought. Could her beach vision have been just that, a thinning, a moment when the barrier between self and soul, past and present, dissolved?

As she read further, psychologists had noted that trauma or powerful emotional states sometimes leave residues that resurface later in life, unbidden, as dreams, sensations, or sudden déjà vu. But across the world, cultures tell stories of children recalling past lives in uncanny detail. In India, Sri Lanka, and parts of North America, researchers like Ian Stevenson had documented hundreds of such cases—children naming towns they had never seen, remembering people they had never met, recounting deaths as if they had never lived.

Science dismissed much of it as coincidence, suggestion, or fabrication. Still, there lingered the possibility that memory was not only neural but cosmic.

Nilima thought back to her own vision. She wasn't merely remembering; she was inhabiting. It was as if a door had opened, and she had stepped through into another layer of reality. Could childhood amnesia explain that? Or had she brushed against something older, something beneath her own lifetime?

Her chest tightened with longing. She wanted to go back to recall more, to unlock what lay beneath the surface of her ordinary life.

So she returned to the beach, again and again. She sat in the same place, at the same hour, even timing her visits with the rhythm of the moon. Yet nothing changed. Only the sea, endless and indifferent, whispered against the shore.

The memories she pulled from her own mind were pale in comparison: a fleeting laugh in her mother's kitchen, her father's hand guiding her across a street, the sting of gravel against her knees after a fall. They were moments, yes—but not revelations. They carried no shimmer, no collapse of time.

Frustration consumed her. Her days became restless searches, trawling the internet for answers. She devoured studies on memory formation, brain plasticity, hypnosis, and past-life regression therapy. She lingered on stories of those who had undergone deep meditation or trance, claiming to recover fragments of another existence. Some spoke of sudden visions that were neither dream nor memories, but something in between.

For hours, she read until her eyes burned, until words blurred across the glowing screen. Article after article, forum after forum. Psychology and spirituality clashed and overlapped, each offering fragments but never the whole picture.

Until, finally, there was nothing left to read.

Nilima sank back in her chair, exhausted. The room hummed with silence. She closed her laptop with a soft, final click, as though she was sealing away her endless search.

And for the first time since the vision, she was left with nothing but the echo of her own questions. Restless, she started to count her breath, deep breathing, as she fell asleep.

Florida March 2020

Garden Of The Mind

Nilima could not rest. Her PCU floor turned into a COVID unit as the influx of COVID-19 patients started to show in Florida. Tomorrow is the first day of change.

When she entered the COVID unit for the first time, Nilima paused at the threshold, taking in the sea of beds separated by thin curtains, the steady beeping of monitors, the muffled coughs, and labored breaths. Every face behind the mask was a story, every patient confined by illness. She pulled on her gloves, adjusted her mask, and approached the first bed.

"Good morning," she said softly; her voice was barely audible above the machines. The patient turned with her eyes wide and frightened. Nilima felt a surge of empathy and determination. Here, she realized, she could ask questions, not for grades or approval, but for understanding, for compassion, for life itself.

Throughout her shift, Nilima moved from bed to bed, checking vitals, administering medications, and offering words of reassurance. Each small gesture, the adjustment of a pillow, a hand held briefly in encouragement, felt monumental. She remembered her childhood, the energy she saw in nature, the stars she had watched, and for a moment, she imagined sending that vibrant energy to those suspended lives in the COVID unit. She also remembered the butterfly lived a short life, as these patients take their last breath.

By the end of the day, her mask left imprints on her face, her back ached from bending and moving quickly, and yet she felt quiet satisfaction. The shortage of masks and gowns didn't bother her. The one-time mask and gown quickly became worn on a weekly basis. At the time of duty, she forgot, this was the kind of presence she had always sought—a way to observe, help, and be of use without pretense.

As she walked out of the unit into the evening light, Nilima felt the city differently. Empty roads, closed shops, and no laughter from the kids on the street. In the quiet of her apartment that night, she traced invisible letters in the air, writing her thoughts as she had always done, whispering silently to the universe: Today, I was here. Today, I mattered.

As she sat on her living room sofa, her mind wandered about memory vs consciousness. She continued her journey of endless research about memory and the connection of brain function. Nilima was logical, and science was always her safeguard. If science proves it, she will accept it. That's always been her motto.

The silence after closing her laptop only deepened her hunger to know more. If science could not give her the answers, perhaps experience itself would.

The research had left her with possibilities: hypnosis, guided meditation, and regression therapy. Some dismissed them as pseudoscience, but others swore by them, claiming that the mind, under the right conditions, could descend into deeper layers of memory, peeling back the veil of childhood amnesia and even touching the remnants of past lives.

She began small breathing exercises. Journaling her dreams each morning before they dissolved into daylight. She sat cross-legged in her living room, eyes closed, whispering mantras she had found in old texts online. At first, nothing came but restless thoughts and the dull ache of sitting too long. But sometimes, in the stillness, there was a flicker, a color, sound, or a scent that did not belong to her present life.

Once, she caught the smell of smoke, sharp, earthy, nothing like her apartment. Another time, she felt the unmistakable black ant bite on her bare feet, though she was sitting on a rug. Sometimes she felt her lungs filled with water as if she were submerged in a body of water. These were not memories she could name, but they were sensations that felt borrowed, as though they had seeped through from another time.

Still, the more she tried to force memory, the more it resisted. Meditation left her restless, frustrated. Guided recordings from the internet only lulled her into shallow sleep. At times, she wondered if she was chasing shadows, inventing meaning where there was none.

And yet there had been the beach. The undeniable immersion. She had not imagined that.

One evening, determined, Nilima set out a plan. If memory were both biology and consciousness, then she would treat it like a door with more than one key. She would try combinations: meditation under moonlight, writing by candle flame, even fasting to sharpen her senses. Somewhere, she believed, the door would open again.

What she feared most was not failure but what she might discover. Because if the memory at the beach had been the beginning of her life—her own, or something she imagined as a false memory—then what would it mean for the life she was currently living?

She pressed her palms together, whispering a silent vow. Memories are not reliable because they can create stories that didn't happen. The brain is lazy, and our evolutionary survival instinct is not always helpful in the modern world.

She would not stop until she found the truth. It happened again….

It happened again; all her senses were highly alert, as if she were moving. She experienced a few moments of her past very vividly and in detail, as if she were there and it were the present time.

Dhaka, Bangladesh 1982-1984:

Kalapuri's Window Seat

Nilima was in her school uniform, a yellow skirt paired with a white shirt, her two pigtails bouncing slightly as she moved. Short for her age, she looked sad, a stark contrast to her mother's excitement as she prepared tiffin for Nilima's sister. "Today is Kala Puri's first day at school," her mother said cheerfully, hoping her daughter would finally receive the education and manners she hadn't been able to instill at home.

The city of Dhaka did not seem right for her, almost claustrophobic. Nilima was not happy. As she, her sister, and mother approached the car, she bolted back inside, locking herself in her room. Frustrated, her mother knocked gently. "Amar shona Kala Puri, enomta kore na, tor school besh valo lagbe," she coaxed. ("Come on, Kala Puri, don't do that, my sweet baby; trust me, you will love school.") Nilima hesitated, then finally emerged, asking softly, "Ma, sotti?" ("You promise?")

Their new home, a two-bedroom flat on the fifth floor with three verandas, felt claustrophobic to Nilima, like a prison. Riding through Dhaka, the city's overwhelming population struck her, the carelessness of people on the streets, and the stark poverty. She saw a young mother in a yellow saree, carrying a baby, while another child, Nilima's age, clutched her hand. When the mother handed the woman some money, Nilima's eyes widened at the sight of so many malnourished children, desperate for shelter. The driver's words, "Madam, apni shobai k deye parben na" ("You can't help everyone"), left Nilima unsettled.

Moving to Dhaka meant confinement; she missed the freedom of her old home, her friends, and her solitary walks in the garden collecting leaves, flowers, and sticks. "When will we go back home?" she asked. "Aitai amader bari akhon theke, Kala Puri!" ("This is our home from now on, Kala Puri!") her mother replied.

School was overwhelming. The classroom buzzed with loud children, and Nilima, quiet and reflective, struggled with the noise. Her teacher assigned seats, and Nilima, relieved, found herself next to a window. But when asked to write her name on the chalkboard, she faltered, unsure of the Bengali and English alphabets. Writing "NIIMA," she read aloud, "Nilima," and was met with laughter. The teacher's scolding and the assignment to write her name a hundred times only deepened her sense of alienation.

She gazed out the window, mesmerized by the sun's rays striking the desk at a perfect 45-degree angle, following them to a tree with birds and a nest. Lost in observation, she barely noticed the teacher's reprimand.

Nilima's academic journey was a constant struggle. Detention, physical punishments, and relentless questioning marked her school life. Despite passing entrance exams with top scores, her performance often placed her at the bottom of her class. She questioned the rigid rules of the schools, the pointless memorization of poems, assigned seating that encouraged the better students to sit at the front, and punishment for curiosity.

Her teachers and mother, unable to explain the purpose, relied on authority and discipline instead. Yet Nilima remained resilient, unafraid to express herself and determined to understand the world on her own terms.

Once she challenged the 3rd-grade teacher and curiously asked, "Why don't you have students like me who are struggling sit on the front bench?"

The teacher replied, "Who makes the rules here?" and then instructed her to do detention after class for 100 squats.

Amid these challenges, Nilima found small heavens of joy. On the rooftop of their building, she explored flowerpots, tasted sun-dried pickles, and watched the night sky.

The stars became her companions, and she often wrote her thoughts in the air, imagining a diary that reached the universe itself. Village visits during school holidays offered even greater freedom, dirt roads, ponds with water lilies, bamboo groves, and starlit nights filled her with awe and contentment. There, she realized she could be a loner without being lonely, at peace with her own thoughts, independent of others' expectations.

Kalapuri's Air Diary

Nilima's inner world—her questions, reflections, and imaginary diary became her sanctuary. In the quiet of her room, under the whir of the ceiling fan, she traced letters in the air with her index finger, practicing her name and imagining her life unfolding in ways only she could shape. She could see the alphabet dance in the air before making words and eventually sentences. She longed for a family and teachers who understood her, her freedom to ask questions without punishment, and her space to observe the world with wonder. "Is that too much to ask?" she whispered silently to the universe, before finally closing her eyes and drifting into dreams of tomorrow's possibilities.

It was report card day. When Nilima was called to receive her report in homeroom, she walked hesitantly towards the teacher, took the paper, and returned to her seat without glancing at it. She already knew the truth: she hadn't done well. The teacher casually mentioned, "Oh, by the way, there is a letter for your parents with the report card." Nilima felt a flutter of apprehension.

The school day dragged on, each tick of the clock amplifying her unease. On the way home, her sister's friend noticed Nilima and asked, "Is that your sister, the girl who gets the most detentions?" The friend's loud curiosity spread quickly, mortifying Nilima's sister, who tried to cover for her by saying, "Oh no, she's just my neighbor, we go home together." The sister's attempt at protection, meant for social pride, wounded Nilima deeply. Once in the car, her sister brusquely pushed her aside and muttered, "Tui amar bon nah holeo parti." (I wish you were not my sister). Nilima remained quiet, a storm of thoughts swirling in her mind. How had she ended up here? Was this family truly hers?

At home, the anxiety only grew. Her father would return from his tour the next day, inevitably asking about the report card. She foresaw the pattern: yelling, disappointment, perhaps even arguments, questioning whether she would ever graduate. Life felt like a predictable calaboose of expectation and reprimand.

Then, the unexpected happened. Her mother read the letter first, and her frustration melted into shock. Nilima had been expelled. The words "Why?" escaped her lips before understanding could settle. Her mother, now incandescent with concern, sobbed, "Kala puri, amar kopal bhanga, tor moto maye k ami kono bhabe parini kichu shikate," (I have failed to teach you anything). She quickly decided to shield her husband from the truth, fearing his reaction.

When her father returned, the family dinner took place under an uneasy quiet. Her sister boasted of being first in class, drawing their father's praise. Then he looked at Nilima. The silence was thick enough to hear a pin drop. Her mother timidly interjected, "Kala puri valo koreche, hoyto first ba second hoi ni, kintu onak chesta kore jano" (She did well, maybe not first or second, but she tried very hard). Nilima, astonished at her father's unusual restraint, could not meet his gaze. Perhaps, she thought, some higher force had intervened.

That night, Nilima returned to her sacred ritual. Extending her hand toward the ceiling, she wrote invisible words in the air, a diary only the stars could read. She poured her thoughts into the sky: the struggles of living with a mother preoccupied by a newborn sibling, her longing for a family where voices spoke in kindness rather than reprimand. Her desire was for teachers who appreciated curiosity over obedience. She closed her diary with the same question she had whispered before sleep: "Is that too much to ask?"

After her father departed for another tour, her mother took decisive action. Dressed in a light green saree, hair neatly in a bun, minimal jewelry, and no makeup, she approached Nilima with a quiet determination. "Come with me," she instructed, her worry visible as they drove in silence to the school. At the principal's office, Nilima waited, listening to the adult conversation she could only partly understand.

The principal, firm in his stance, initially refused to readmit Nilima. However, her mother, invoking the successes of her older daughter, pleaded for leniency. After a tense pause, the principal finally offered a solution: a payment of 20,000 taka as a silent arrangement to secure

Nilima's place at the school. Relief washed over her mother; she had managed to navigate the system without burdening her husband.

Back home, she clasped Nilima's hand and said gently, "Kala puri, tui akhon theke valo kore pora shuna korbi, Kemon?" (From now on, you will concentrate on your studies. All I ask is that you pass your classes. Okay?)

Nilima nodded, understanding not just the practical necessity but the subtle lesson: survival often required both courage and strategy, and her diary in the air would continue to hold the truths her voice could not yet share.

Kalapuri's Invisible Pen

As Nilima lay in her bed that night, the ceiling fan cast slow, rhythmic shadows across the room, and her thoughts lifted her beyond the four walls. The words she traced in the air—her invisible diary—were not merely letters, but prayers, questions, and quiet affirmations of her existence. Each stroke of her finger was a tether to something larger than herself, a bridge between her small, imperfect world and the vastness of the sky.

She wondered if the universe was listening, if the stars themselves could understand the longing and confusion of a child trapped in a world that often misunderstood her. "Is it too much to ask," she whispered silently, "To be seen, to be understood, to belong?" Her voice carried only in the stillness, yet it felt heard. In that quiet communion, Nilima discovered a subtle truth: the act of naming her thoughts, of giving shape to her questions, was itself a form of power.

In her mind's eye, she saw her life as a series of interconnected moments, each like a bead strung along an invisible thread. She could not yet explain why she felt drawn to watch the ant's tunnel or butterflies' nest, or why the most minor details of the world sparked wonder in her heart. But she sensed that these seemingly trivial observations were sacred, and that the universe was teaching her patience, attentiveness, and reverence for all living things.

Her air diary became a sanctuary where judgment and fear could not reach her. No one can find it and read it. No one can make fun of her. The air diary was her only friend, as she was never able to make friends at school. Here, she could fail, explore, and question without punishment. And in that invisible space, she began to feel a gentle, unwavering presence guiding her—a sense that even when the world was harsh, she was never truly alone.

Nilima realized that her spirit could travel far beyond her small body, beyond her school or family, beyond the narrow expectations imposed upon her. In this sacred inner space, she discovered freedom: the freedom to wonder, to dream, to fail, and to rise again. Each night, as her finger danced in the air, she stitched together a tapestry of understanding, curiosity, and quiet courage—a spiritual reservoir she could draw from when the world seemed heavy or unkind.

By the time her eyelids grew heavy and sleep claimed her, Nilima's heart was lighter. Her diary had brought her closer to herself, closer to the universe, and closer to a wisdom she did not yet have words for. And as she drifted, she whispered one final thought into the quiet: "Even if no one else understands me, I will always understand myself."

Pickles And Petals

It was a few months later, and spring had just arrived. The morning showers and the gentle afternoon breeze filled Nilima with quiet happiness. On weekends, when everyone was busy with chores, she would sneak up to the rooftop, a five-story escape that had become her sanctuary. The rooftop was ordinary in many ways: pots of flowers and plants lined the edges, and people hung their clothes to dry in the sun. Yet for Nilima, it was a world of her own.

She always carried a little plate and a spoon, hidden beneath her dress. Pickles were her delight, a small stolen joy from the ten flats shared by the building. Each household displayed its pickles in the sun, drying and fermenting with care. Nilima told herself, "If I taste the pickles, I can help them improve their cooking. I'm not stealing; I'm helping." She took only a spoonful at a time, savoring the flavors, commenting on textures, and gently critiquing in her mind. Some neighbors even encouraged her, sending extra pickles her way. When her mother discovered this little ritual, she was disappointed, and Nilima eventually stopped practicing it.

The rooftop was not only a place for secret indulgence, but it was also her observatory. At sunset and under the blanket of night, she would climb up with her aunt and siblings to watch the stars. Springtime brought a sweet, gentle breeze from the north and flowers in full bloom, a spectacle that never failed to fill her with awe. Looking at her younger self, Nilima realized she had always been a loner, yet she was never lonely. She found contentment in her own thoughts and space. Although people were around her constantly, she never felt the need to cultivate deeper connections, unlike her sister, who was inseparable from their aunt, or her younger brother, who clung to their mother.

Nilima noticed small patterns of belonging and difference within her family. Her brother adored certain foods, and she always saved the best pieces for him. Her sister, on the other hand, demanded lavish birthday celebrations and trendy clothes, while Nilima cared little for such ceremonies. Birthdays were just another day to her, indistinguishable from the rise of the sun, the flight of birds, or the flow of the river to the ocean. When her mother surprised her on her seventh birthday, she refused to cut the cake or take pictures, angry that the day had been arranged without her consent. She could not explain why she felt this way; it was simply her nature.

From a young age, Nilima took ownership of her life. She spoke her mind freely and was never fearful of expressing her ideas, even when her school punishments were harsh. Detentions and scoldings did not deter her; she showed up the next day with a smile, undaunted. She forgot things easily, held no grudges, and yet she remained unwavering in her convictions. Her vision, her ideas, mattered above all else.

On that rooftop, surrounded by flowers, sunlight, and the whisper of the wind, Nilima felt an unmistakable sense of freedom. She belonged, not to anyone or anything else, but to herself.

Dancing Fish And Mystic Pond

Every year during the holidays, when school was off for two weeks, the family traveled to the village where her grandfather lived. They would meet with other uncles and aunts at the train station and journey together. Nilima always awaited this trip eagerly; the village vacation was the highlight of her year. It took roughly six hours to reach Sylhet from Dhaka, followed by another two-hour car ride to the village.

Nilima loved it there. At a certain point, the car could no longer go forward—the dirt roads were narrow, and she would swing herself out, running towards the village. As she walked, she passed a pond. Children bathed at one corner, and women washed clothes at the other. The pond always fascinated her, yet it frightened her too; she had heard of her second cousin drowning there at five years old. Water, she thought, could be both comforting and terrifying.

The stairs in the village fascinated her as well, huge slabs of stone, uneven, carved by hand. Nilima preferred the imperfection and naturalness of it to the rigid, processed steps of Dhaka. To her left, bamboo trees swayed, and to her right, a small guest house with a tin roof, wooden door, and shuttered windows appeared. She loved the simplicity and charm of it. After passing the guest house, she climbed a few more steps and descended into a vast courtyard surrounded by tin-roofed houses with wrap-around verandas. The kitchen stood far behind, and she ran freely, exploring every corner.

She adored everything about this village—the food, the trees, the dirt roads, the walkways, and especially the night. Without city lights or the noise of cars, the nights were darker than coals, and the sounds of nature came alive. Fireflies lit up the darkness, and stars shimmered brighter than she had ever seen. She and her cousins would run and play, while the adults lingered under the open sky, lost in endless conversation.

Nilima kept a diary in her imagination. She recorded her observations: the people selling boiled eggs at train stations, the disabled beggars asking for coins, and the comings and goings of passengers. Her diary, she felt, was safe in the universe, invisible to prying eyes, yet forever preserved. It made her free.

One morning, awakened by a rooster's crow, Nilima noticed her cousins were still sleeping. She opened the door and stepped outside, only to hear her grandfather's voice: "Kala puri Nilima, hattbi amar shate." (Come walk with me, Nilima). They strolled through the village, exploring chicken coops, jackfruit trees, mango trees, and rice fields. Hours later, they arrived at a cemetery. A pond, surrounded by red walls, marked its entrance. Her grandfather recounted a legend: every burial added a fish to the pond. It originally started with only one. Nilima peered into the water and could see only herself at first. "Dadabhai, mach nai" (Grandfather, there are no fish), she cried.

Her grandfather advised patience. "Kala puri," he said softly, "Sometimes, you have to look slowly, really look, to see what is happening around you."

Nilima sat down at the edge of the pond, her small legs dangling over the red-walled steps. She peered into the water, frowning. "But I don't see anything, Dadabhai," she said, her voice tinged with impatience.

"Be patient, child," he replied with a gentle smile. "Look closer. Life moves differently than we expect."

Gradually, shapes began to emerge, hundreds of black and silver fish moving in hypnotic, circular patterns near the pond's bottom. They were not merely swimming; they seemed to be performing a silent dance, each movement purposeful, each turn part of a larger, unspoken rhythm.

Nilima's eyes widened. "They're… dancing," she whispered, mesmerized.

"Yes," her grandfather said, nodding. "And they are not alone. See how they move together? Each one depends on the other, just like us."

Nilima took a long look at the fish and discovered that all the fish stopped moving and looked at her. She, too, continued to look back at them. One of the fish swam up and said, "Shongjoge shanti, alingone bhalobasha"—a Bengali phrase she didn't understand. The fish repeated three times, but she could not understand. She called Dada Bhai to show him, but when he looked, the fish returned to the circular motion.

Dada bhai said, "It is very captivating to watch them", without understanding what Nilima was referring to.

"The water… it moves with them, too," Nilima murmured, tracing the patterns with her finger in the air. "They're not just in the pond, they are part of it."

Her grandfather chuckled softly. "Exactly. Every creature, every plant, every gust of wind, every drop of water—they all belong to one family, Kala puri. The world is connected, even if we can't always see the threads."

Nilima leaned closer, her hand hovering above the water. "Like the ants at home, or the butterflies in the garden?" she asked.

"Exactly like them," her grandfather replied, "Even the breeze brushing the bamboo is part of the same story. Life flows, and each of us has a role to play in it."

She gazed at the fish swimming in hypnotic circles, imagining herself mirrored in their motion. "I think… I think I'm part of it too, Dadabhai," she said softly, a mixture of awe and wonder in her voice.

Her grandfather squeezed her hand. "You are, Kala puri. We are never truly separate. Look at the leaves, the birds, the water, everything is alive, and everything is connected."

Nilima's brow furrowed as a new thought arose. "Dadabhai… what happens when someone dies? Do they disappear? Are they still part of the world, like the fish?"

Her grandfather paused, watching the fish with her. "Ah, death… It is a change, Kala puri, not an end. The body goes, but the spirit, the energy… it flows into the world, into everything around us. Like the fish, they may vanish from sight, but their essence joins the rhythm of life. You see, the river does not hold water forever—it flows, it moves, it nourishes everything along its path. Life is much the same."

Nilima looked at him, absorbing his words. "So… my grandmother… she is in the trees, in the bamboo, in the wind?"

"Yes, child. In every sound, every smell, every living thing. When you listen carefully, you will hear her. When you watch closely, you will see her. She is never truly gone."

In that moment, Nilima felt a quiet sense of humility and deep reverence. Life was not a collection of separate beings; it was a single, living organism with countless expressions. Birds called from the treetops, leaves rustled like whispers, insects hummed their constant songs, and her own heartbeat and breath became part of the rhythm.

"Will the fish always be here, Dadabhai?" she asked, gazing back at the pond.

"Perhaps," he said. "Or perhaps they will change. But the rhythm of life continues, just as it should. We are part of it, and it is part of us."

Nilima felt her small hand tighten around his, and for the first time, she understood in her bones that even in death, there is continuity. All living things, seen and unseen, are threads in the same tapestry.

Back at the house, breakfast was served: red sticky rice, an egg omelet, and vegetable curry. Nilima noticed that food always tasted better in the village—the eggs, milk, vegetables, and fish seemed more genuine somehow. Suddenly, her father suggested a boat ride tomorrow. Mother hesitated but eventually agreed.

The Ripples Of Fate

The next morning, everyone was prepared to enjoy a day on the boat. The children set off with their father and uncle in a country boat, a simple wooden Balami Nouka crafted with skill. There were six of them, cousins and three uncles.

The morning sun hung low but bright, casting its light on every leaf, every brick, and every puddle in a palette of vibrant colors. Nilima walked alongside her cousins, noticing the narrow dirt road, the cool breeze on her face, and the music played in the trees; everyone was busy carrying on conversations.

They walked by a pond, its surface sparkling like a glass in the sunlight. Come on, where are the frogs and fish games, and what are these flooded cities across the calm surface? The white petals were so bright and unfurling as if greeting the sun. Nilima paused, noticing small wonders beyond everyday life, when she heard someone say, "Cholo kalapuri."

Continuing along the road that led downward toward the river, she noticed some shops and beautifully crafted boats of different shapes and sizes.

Finally, she reached the riverbank. The water glimmered under the brilliant sunlight, reflecting the sky like liquid glass, with gentle waves lapping against the mud-streaked shore. The boat waited patiently, a humble Balami Nouka crafted from polished local wood, its curved hull perfect for slicing through the calm water. A small hood made of woven bamboo offered shade, and six little seats fit snugly beneath it. The craftsmanship spoke of generations, with each nail and joint carefully placed, a vessel both sturdy and alive with history.

Nilima stepped onto the boat, gripping the smooth wood with reverent fingers. As it floated into the river, the current carried them along, and the cool breeze kissed her face. She leaned over the edge, letting her hand skim the water's surface, sending gentle ripples across her reflection.

The river seemed to breathe with her, alive and adaptable, moving effortlessly around the obstacles in its path. Sunlight danced on the gentle waves, and dragonflies skimmed just above, their wings catching tiny rainbows as they zipped across the surface.

The farther they went, the more the village shrank behind them, and the river widened into a shining silver ribbon. Trees bent over the bank, their roots tangled with the earth, whispering stories of centuries past.

Birds called to each other, and in the distance, the faint, rhythmic splash of another boat mingled with the river's gentle murmur. Nilima felt a thrill of freedom, a rare sense of being both small and part of something immense, where the warmth of the sun, the scent of the river, and the boat's gentle rocking made her heart expand with wonder.

The boat glided gently over the shimmering river, and Nilima leaned over the edge, dipping her small fingers into the water. "Look, Baba! The river… it moves everywhere, but never stops!" she exclaimed, her eyes sparkling.

Her father smiled, steadying the boat. "Yes, Nilima, water adapts… it flows with everything, yet it never loses itself."

But the sky darkened quickly. Clouds churned above, and the wind whispered warnings through the bamboo lining the shore. The river became restless, with waves splashing against the boat with sudden urgency.

"Nilima, sit down!" her father called, voice tight with concern.

"I don't want to! I want to see!" she shouted, gripping the edge.

The boat rocked violently, tossing the children around like leaves in a storm. The river seemed alive, roaring beneath her. Nilima's small body wobbled, and before anyone could reach her, the boat tipped over. She plunged into the cold, chaotic water.

"Nilima!" her father yelled, diving after her. Her arms flailed, mouth opening and closing as she swallowed the river. Panic took her breath.

"Hold on, Kala puri! Don't fight it!" her uncle shouted, plunging in from the other side.

The whirlpool's pull was merciless, dragging her beneath the boat as though the river itself had decided to claim her. Water rushed into her ears, her eyes, and her very breath, spinning her into a dizzying spiral of darkness. Panic erupted inside her chest—fear so sharp it threatened to shatter her completely. She struggled against the current, but it was stronger, endless, a living force that would not let her go.

Then, in the blur of her terror, Nilima saw them.

The Fish.

The same ones from the pond—glimmering black and silver bodies moving in perfect circles, their dance both wild and ordered, like a secret ritual performed beneath the surface. As she watched, the panic in her chest softened, as if their rhythmic motion spoke directly to her heartbeat. Their circles mirrored the whirlpool itself, but theirs was not chaos, just harmony. In their spinning, she felt not death but peace—an unspoken assurance that even in the pull of the unknown, there could be calm.

One by one, the fish stilled. Their movements ceased, and the waters around her seemed to pause, as though waiting for a message. Then one fish swam forward, its mouth opening—not with bubbles, but with words.

"Shongjoge shanti, alingone bhalobasha."

The sound vibrated through her body more than her ears, resonating in her bones, in the very core of her being. For a moment, she was weightless, suspended in the river's womb, carried not by fear but by something sacred.

And then—suddenly—they were gone. The fish dissolved into the current as if they had never been there at all. The river roared back to life, tugging at her again, and the panic returned. But before despair could take her, she felt it—hands.

Strong, steady hands.

They gripped her arms with certainty, with human warmth, breaking the cold dominion of the water. With a force greater than the current, they pulled her upward—out of the spiral, out of the fear, out of the river's fury.

She gasped for air as the surface split open above her, lungs burning but alive. She coughed violently, water choking her lungs, shivering as she gulped in air.

Her father held her tightly, eyes wide with relief. "Do you understand now, Nilima? Respect the river… its strength… its unpredictability."

Nilima, trembling, clung to him and whispered hoarsely, "I… I didn't mean to…"

"You are alive," her father said, voice breaking slightly. "That's what matters. Never forget that even beauty can be dangerous, and even fear can teach you something."

The sky wept above them, rain drenching their hair and clothes, but Nilima felt a strange clarity settle in her chest. She had glimpsed the raw power of nature and survived.

The rest of the vacation was spent resting. Days in bed felt like years to Nilima. She scribbled in her imaginary diary about the bamboo trees, fruit trees, and endless night skies she would miss. She wrote about survival, wondering why we live, what makes life precious, and where the answers might be found. One evening, the moonlight slipped through the shutters, illuminating her small form. She rested her hand on her stomach and drifted into sleep, comforted by its silver glow.

The village had taught her wonder and fear, freedom and reflection. She carried the dancing fish, the hidden stories, and the open skies in her mind, shaping her inner world forever.

Back To Dhaka And Back To School….

The mother received a phone call from the school stating that Nilima is out of breath and has an uncontrollable, non-productive cough. The teacher also mentioned that she has been coughing since she started school a couple of days ago, and seemed very tired. Today, she was suddenly unable to breathe…

Nilima's mother took her to the PG hospital, her heart pounding. Admitted to the ICU, and after 12 hours, the mother was able to see her.

The ICU was cold and bright, filled with the steady beeping of machines and the sharp smell of antiseptic. Nurses moved quickly, attending to patients. Nilima lay on the bed, pale and weak, with tubes in her arms and an oxygen mask on her face. Her cough rattled her chest, and each breath seemed like a struggle.

Her mother knelt beside her. "Amar maye…" (My little one) she whispered, tears streaming down her cheeks.

A doctor approached, holding Nilima's chest X-ray. "Mrs. Chowdhury, Nilima has aspiration pneumonia. Both lungs have fluid, probably from the near-drowning in the village," he explained.

Her mother's voice trembled. "Near-drowning… my baby… what will happen?"

"She was lucky," the doctor said quietly. "Many young children who fall into water like this don't survive. The danger is very real, and her body was under severe stress. Oxygen levels drop quickly, and infections can set in afterward."

Her mother gasped, gripping Nilima's hand tightly. "I… I thought I lost her."

"Accidental deaths like this are sadly common among children," the doctor continued. "Even small moments—falling into water, choking, accidents at home—can become life-threatening. Parents often feel helpless, but immediate care can save them."

Nilima, unconscious, seemed to sense her mother's worry and love. Her adult self-remembered watching her mother pray, whispering hopes and blessings as she tried to keep fear at bay. Though Nilima wasn't religious, she felt the power of her mother's love as if it were giving her strength, connecting her body to the care surrounding her.

Her mother's hands shook. "Doctor… will she survive?"

"She is resilient," the doctor said. "Her body is strong, and with oxygen, antibiotics, and close monitoring, she will recover. Your presence, your care, your calm, all this helps her fight."

Her mother held Nilima's tiny hand close to her heart. "Tui bachbi, kala puri… You will live."

Days passed in a blur of oxygen masks, IVs, and monitor beeps. Nilima's small body struggled, but gradually, she began breathing easier. Her mother whispered encouragement, adjusted blankets, and offered water, staying close every moment.

One day, the doctor checked in and said, "Mrs. Chowdhury, many children like Nilima face accidents, but her recovery is a testament to her resilience and the care she is receiving. Children's bodies can heal in remarkable ways if given support."

Nilima opened her eyes slightly and saw her mother's tear-streaked face. She reached up, touching her mother's cheek. Though she could not speak, they shared a silent understanding: fear, love, and hope intertwined.

At times, the family thought she might not make it this time. Nilima doesn't remember the few days when she was upscaled to the ICU. However, as a witness to herself as an adult, Nilima struggled to survive, and many days, her mother prayed that she would get better.

Nilima wanted to comfort her mother, but realized she couldn't be seen or heard. It is incredible how we get scared of the unknown, she thought. The unpredictable future brings people closer to God out of fear. Nilima is not religious and grew up in a household where religion wasn't imposed on the kids.

Although her mother would try to teach from time to time, Nilima and her siblings weren't tied to any concrete ideas of any religion. Now that she is looking at her mother, praying to God seems irrelevant. The treatment and the body's response to the treatment are the determining factors for my survival, she thought. Or perhaps mother's blessing and prayers helped Nilima to gain strength and overcome pneumonia.

In her view, the blessing helped the mother to get positive energy and improved her overall care for Nilima. She grew up hearing the story that "Kala Puri survived miraculously and came back from near-death experiences."

Honestly, Nilima considered the true "miracles" in her multiple near-death experiences to be purely biological. She marveled at the resilience of her body—how her cells had rallied, repairing damage, fighting infection, and keeping life against overwhelming odds. Her survival wasn't the result of divine intervention, but rather the remarkable, almost hidden capabilities of the human body itself.

She saw herself fighting for every breath, saw her mother's desperate prayers and trembling hands. She wanted to help, to comfort, and to whisper that she would survive—but she could not. No one could see her, no one could hear her. She was trapped in the awareness of helplessness, a witness to her own childhood fear and fragility. And in that moment, she felt a deep, aching understanding of what it means to be small and powerless.

Florida July 2020

Fragments Of Memories

A few months passed by, and all she is doing is working and coming home, away from the outside world. She never watches TV. Sometimes she watches movies with the kids, but they haven't been to her place for a while. One night, Nilima woke in her bed, repeating the phrase "Shongjoge shanti, alingone bhalobasha", blinking against the soft, golden morning light that spilled through the half-open window. The smell of fresh linen mixed with the faint scent of jasmine from the garden outside. Was it a dream? Despite the rest, she felt no more refreshed than before. Her body was heavy, her limbs reluctant, and her mind felt suspended between moments, caught in fragments of memory she could almost touch but couldn't fully grasp.

She had fallen out of time again, as if her mind was playing tricks, remembering things that had never been told to her yet refusing to summon them when she tried. The distant hum of the city outside, children laughing in the courtyard below, and the soft flutter of curtains in the morning breeze all seemed both familiar and unreal.

"Shongjoge shanti, alingone bhalobasha."

Strange—she had never heard this phrase before, and she couldn't even grasp its meaning completely. How could it be possible that the fish spoke? Or that the encounter had truly happened at all? Could there have been another fish of the same kind drifting in the river's current, carrying this same hidden message? None of it made sense to her, at least not in the ordinary way.

Later, she discovered the translation: "In connection, there is peace; in embrace, there is love." The words lingered within her like a riddle, whispering of truths beyond logic. She had no clue what this had to do with her—unless it was a reflection of her own solitude, the aching silence of being cut off from friends, and the distance from family that weighed on her spirit.

Perhaps, she thought, this was no madness at all, but rather the river itself speaking through the living symbols it carried. Maybe the phrase was not meant to be understood by the mind but received by the soul—a reminder that peace is not found in isolation, but in the weaving together of hearts; that love reveals itself not in thought, but in the sacred act of embrace.

She tried to rationalize it, yet reason felt like sand slipping through her fingers. The experience was not meant to be concrete—it was meant to be felt. A message from beyond, calling her to remember that even in solitude, she is never truly alone. Connection flows like the river; love breathes in every current; and the divine speaks in ways she may never fully understand, but recognizes that there was such memory.

Why would an eight-year-old Nilima have this experience? She had no clue of the words; rest assured, the meaningful phrase. Also, if it was not real, then why did I travel to those specific memories of mine? It is not real, or was it? How are we supposed to believe everything we hear or see, as many things can be false memories. As psychology says, "Don't believe everything your mind tells you, learn the truth!"

Then she thought, her recent separation from her husband, working as a COVID nurse with death and destruction, and not being able to have the children over her apartment due to fear of infection from her—all of it seemed to swirl in her mind like leaves caught in a river's current, unsettling yet strangely grounding.

Just yesterday, Nilima had two patients die, cared for them, and talked to family members after. It's different to see someone not moving and communicating. Nilima had learned long ago that nursing was not only about preserving life—it was also about honoring it in death. After a patient dies, especially during COVID, it carries its own profound responsibility: to care for the deceased with dignity, to support grieving families, and to navigate protocols born of necessity.

The patient lay still on the bed, her body quiet but heavy with the weight of recent struggle. With help from the Patient Care Technician (PCT), Nilima moved with purpose and care. She first assessed and disconnected all medical devices: IV lines, central lines, catheters, and any drains. Each connection required attention, not only to ensure hospital protocol was followed, but to preserve the patient's dignity in the final moments.

The monitor, once a steady companion of beeps and numbers, had no further purpose. Nilima gently powered it down. The room fell into an almost sacred silence, interrupted only by the muffled sounds of the hospital outside.

Next came the intimate work of cleaning the body. Wearing full PPE, Nilima prepared warm wipes, a basin of soap, and fresh linens. They cleaned the patient's body thoroughly: wiping the face, smoothing the hair, washing the hands, and ensuring the body was free of bodily fluids. She adjusted the hospital gown, tucked the sheets neatly, and positioned the body with care—small gestures that preserved dignity when life had departed.

Once the body was cleaned, Nilima began the process required for COVID-positive decedents. She carefully placed the patient in a sealed body bag, ensuring the zipper was secured and all identifying information was tagged accurately. This was not only hospital protocol but a necessary measure to prevent contamination and ensure safety for everyone involved.

When she attempted to transport the patient to the morgue, she faced an unexpected obstacle: the morgue was full. There was no space for the new arrival. Nilima remained calm, knowing she would have to escalate. She called the house supervisor, explaining the situation:

"This is Nilima from the COVID floor. I have a deceased COVID patient here, bagged and tagged, ready for transport, but the morgue has no available space. Can you assist?"

The house supervisor's voice was calm and assuring.

"Leave the patient in the hallway near the elevator for now. We'll arrange space in the morgue immediately. I will make sure it is taken care of."

Following the instructions, Nilima carefully moved the body to the designated hallway space, among other COVID-deceased patients. Even in this impersonal location, she took a moment to straighten the sheet, adjust the body's position, and ensure that it was treated with respect. The hallway, lined with the silent evidence of the pandemic, was heavy with sorrow, yet each gesture of care preserved the humanity of those who had passed.

Nilima stepped back, reflecting on the magnitude of the work. Post-death care was more than protocol; it was ethical responsibility, humanism, and compassion in action. She knew the families were grieving, and there were many calls for updates and sharing the funeral home information. Each conversation she would have with them required honesty, empathy, and guidance through incomprehensible loss.

In that quiet, she found the essence of nursing: presence. Presence for the living, presence for the dying, and presence for those who had passed. Each life she touched, each patient she guided through final moments, was a reminder that dignity and care transcend the boundary between life and death.

As the house supervisor assured her that the patient would be taken to the morgue as soon as space was available, Nilima felt the weight lift slightly, replaced by the quiet fulfillment that she had done everything possible to honor the patient. This was nursing in its purest form: ethical, compassionate, and unwavering.

As she remembers sitting at home, paradoxically, she never felt more herself. Now her mind is wandering about recent memories. Married for twenty years, she had chosen to part ways, a decision both anticipated and resisted. Marriage had never been her natural path, yet she had entered one at the age of twenty through an arranged union.

In the early months, she admired his honesty, simplicity, and thoughtful gestures. Flowers left at her library desk, his quiet waiting outside to see her, and small acts that made her feel recognized, cherished, and alive.

But, like all living things, nothing remained static. Cells transformed, seasons shifted, and so did the fabric of her life. Permanent, she realized, was an illusion; impermanence was the only constant. The reasons for her separation were hers alone, subtle yet impactful, and she had chosen not to reveal them even to her parents until the finality was certain.

What followed her decision was unexpected and jarring. Members of her Bengali community, assuming authority over her private life, questioned her morality, her devotion, and even her integrity as a mother. One so-called friend demanded she explain herself to the community, as if anyone could understand her unique experiences. Nilima was stunned by the insularity and judgmental mindset she encountered. They lived in a cocoon, rigid and unyielding, oblivious to the transformations of life.

She thought of the butterflies, how they would metamorphose from larvae to cocoon to their winged freedom, unbounded by the limitations of others' perceptions. The image brought a quiet smile to her lips. She could almost feel the warmth of the sun on her wings, the delicate brush of air lifting her higher, untethered from the petty judgments of those around her. People in the community had no decency to feel anything but judgment. In this short life, people have lost empathy, an emotion that is as ancient as dispassion. Perhaps the higher thought of empathy never really existed in the majority.

The barrage of accusations momentarily rattled her, but deep down, she knew the truth: the physical presence or absence of someone did not define the essence of a relationship. True connections were mental, spiritual, subtle, stretching across distances as easily as they did through proximity. She could sense it in the quiet of the room, in the rhythm of her heartbeat, in the laughter of children she cared for.

Nilima could not articulate her experiences fully, nor place them neatly into words, but she knew she must remember them. The threads of her memory stretched back past her seventh year, fragments of a self that had always observed, questioned, and survived. She could feel the weight of the years on her body—the tension in her shoulders, the slow rhythm of her breathing —but she also felt the lightness of her mind, the expansive clarity of her memory.

The rustle of leaves outside, the distant cooing of a bird chirping, and the warmth of sunlight on her arms —all reminded her that life continues, impermanent and fragile, yet filled with small, luminous moments of freedom and clarity. And as she lay back, absorbing the quiet, she resolved to hold onto those threads—to keep recollecting, reflecting, and existing within the fragile, beautiful impermanence of life, letting the fragments of time shape her, teach her, and guide her forward. As she transcends…

The New Horizon

Dhaka, 1990

Nilima was twelve years old. The apartment was empty, and the luggage was packed, the walls echoing with the quiet hum of anticipation. Her father meticulously checked every passport, ticket, and document. They were about to immigrate to America, sponsored by her aunt, a journey that promised hope but also uncertainty.

It was Nilima's first airplane ride, and the thought of soaring above the clouds made her both thrilled and terrified. From the hushed conversations of her parents, she gathered that her father was reluctant to leave, even though he kept an open mind. While her mother brimmed with excitement, dreaming of a better future.

The moment the plane started moving down the runway, fear gripped Nilima. Her stomach twisted, her head spun, and the unfamiliar sensation of flying made her feel sick. The long journey stretched endlessly, and every hour was a test of patience and courage.

Alta Loma, California, 1990

The family of five, with ten suitcases brimming with possessions, and hearts heavy with hope, arrived in a land that promised opportunity but delivered culture shock. Although her aunt welcomed them warmly, her cousins were less enthusiastic. The clash of different habits and expectations left a bitter taste in Nilima's mouth.

She remembered vividly how her cousins were so thrilled to see them, and now they avoided them. Nilima wondered, How am I different from them? She asked her mother if she and her siblings had been vaccinated before leaving Bangladesh. "Ha, Kalapuri. Keno?" her mother replied calmly. Nilima wanted to cry out in frustration, to scream at the injustice of it all, but the words were caught in her throat. Instead, she murmured, "Kichu na, Ma," (nothing important).

She longed to return to Khulna, to the freedom of the outdoors, quiet streets, and the company of nature. Back there, there was no society to navigate, no constant judgments. Her mother's dream of a better life in America, she realized, already felt fragile.

In the first few days, Nilima wandered around the backyard for hours, studying the plants her aunt had planted. The weather was perfect, the sun was radiant, and the dirt was clean. Yet everything felt artificial. The perfection of the world unsettled her, and a hollow emptiness tugged at her heart. Even the beauty of the surroundings couldn't fill the space of what she had left behind.

At night, she wrote in her diary, comparing her new home and memories of her father's village to the rooftop of her flat in Dhaka. She missed the simple, imperfect joys of home: the uneven staircases, the bamboo leaves brushing in the wind, the water lilies clinging to the edges of the pond, and the quiet companionship of her grandfather.

Before sleep, her mind turned over larger questions. Why do things happen in people's lives? How do today's decisions shape tomorrow? How would the choice to leave Bangladesh for America change her future?

Nilima and her siblings started school while staying at their aunt's house. The aunt had equipped them with information the day before, including the location of the school bus stop, the bus number to take from school, and the school schedule.

The first day of school was awkward. She was wearing a dress she had brought from Bangladesh, two ponytails, and socks with tennis shoes. As she entered the first classroom, students whispered and laughed. She quietly moved to the last seat and sat down, her eyes fixed on the ground. Her heartbeat was faster than she could count, and she could hear her breathing loud, like whistles.

Someone came over and said, "Hi. Where are you from?" Nilima relaxed a little, thinking, It will be okay. Someone already wants to be my friend.

"Hi, I am from Asia," she replied.

The girl looked at her skeptically—tall, with buttercream skin, eyes blue like the ocean, and hair like golden sand. "You are not from Asia; you are from Africa! Your eyes and your skin color say so." She pushed

Nilima's notebooks off the table. The whole class laughed. Nilima looked up—she was the only dark-skinned student in the room.

Kicking the notebooks aside, she bent down to pick them up, heart racing. Luckily, the teacher entered. Unknowingly, Nilima stood, but realizing no one else had, she sat back down. The teacher introduced her to the class and informed them that her classroom would be different tomorrow.

At lunch, a boy poured milk on her food tray, ruining her lunch. The day dragged on, each moment a struggle. She hardly spoke or thought. Riding the school bus home, her heart was heavy with sorrow, but she couldn't cry. Life seemed to move in one direction—downward. She had never felt so diminished, so unwanted. She didn't know who she was or if she even wanted to be herself anymore.

Meanwhile, at home, her mother grew worried because her brother had not returned from school. It was almost 4 p.m. when her mother called her aunt. They drove around, searching. By 6 p.m., they still hadn't found him. Finally, they realized he had taken the bus to the next neighborhood. There he was, sitting on the sidewalk, crying, with his bookbag on the ground, pants wet, shivering with fear.

That moment was excruciating for Nilima. Seeing his tears, hearing his labored breaths, the long, endless crying, it was almost unbearable. Later, lying close to her sister, mother, and brother, Nilima felt a deep uncertainty about life, mistrust of people, and a questioning of the purpose. The quietness of that room felt suffocating, like walking a foggy morning trail where no birds sang, the breeze was absent, and the sun struggled through a thick fog. She couldn't write in her diary that night; words and feelings had deserted her.

They stayed another week at her aunt's house, but school remained the same. Bullying persisted daily, about her clothes, hairstyle, or something she said. In the last few days, she began taking her lunch to the restroom, sitting on a stool to eat in private. Then, for the first time, she cried. She cried intensely, pounding her hands while resting her head against the bathroom door.

She lost interest in the outside world. She didn't want to look at the stars at night or the plants surrounding her aunt's house. Because her aunt's husband grew increasingly angry with their stay, her mother called her brother to take them home. Nilima thought that staying in Dhaka meant the teacher's punishment for academics; here, punishment was for the way she looked and the way she spoke.

She realized she could not change her skin tone; it would always be brown. Her hair would always be black and curly, and her lips large. Even if she wore what others wore, she would still be Nilima, still speak the exact words.

Then she had a thought that brought a ray of sunlight through the clouds: if she could find just one friend—one who didn't see her color as a burden-and didn't question her origin, that friend could show her purpose, and be her mentor, her cheerleader, her comfort.

That realization overwhelmed her with warmth and light. Nilima understood: she was enough. She was within herself. She was Nilima.

Los Angeles, California 1991-1992

Unbroken

Their uncle lived in a townhome about fifteen miles from Los Angeles. He was married with one infant child. Nilima and her family were warmly welcomed there. Within a few weeks, her mother took over household duties—cooking, cleaning, and caring for the child—while her parents simultaneously searched tirelessly for jobs. Her father went to numerous interviews. Despite extensive experience in civil engineering, her father was either considered too experienced for positions or unfamiliar with the required computer systems.

Her parents often discussed returning home, but her mother was adamant about staying in the States. One evening, as they sat in the small living room, the conversation flared again.

"We've been here almost a year, and your job prospects are bleak," her father said, rubbing his temples. "Maybe we should go back. Bangladesh needs you, and we'll have a life there."

Her mother shook her head firmly. "No, we cannot go back now. The children have adjusted, the schools are good, and I am determined to work. There is opportunity here—we have to find it."

"But every day I go to interviews, and they don't even call me back! I don't belong here, not yet," her father protested.

"Don't you see?" her mother countered, her voice soft but steady. "This is where they can grow, where they can have a future. I won't let you take that from them because it's uncomfortable for you. We are staying."

He looked at her, frustration mixed with admiration. "You're stubborn, you know that?"

"I'm determined," she said, a small smile breaking through. "And someday, you'll see that staying here is the right choice. We'll manage. We always do."

Meanwhile, Nilima and her siblings adjusted well in school, finding peers from other countries or children of first-generation immigrants.

Nilima remembered weekends in downtown LA. Her father would pack homework and food, and they would take the bus early, arriving after an hour-long ride. Every Saturday, being outdoors felt like home. The park fascinated her—the birds singing while she did homework, squirrels darting off during lunch, and she felt the grass under her bare feet while playing tag. On rainy days, they would visit the public library, and every outing would end with a stop at the open market. She wrote endlessly about LA and the park in her diary.

One thought, however, haunted her: some people made the outdoors their permanent home—sleeping under trees or benches. Why did a first-world country have people living like those in the third world? What if her family ended up like them? Her prayers were constant, written in the air, as she hoped God would hear, though she sometimes doubted His capacity to help everyone. Exhausted by confusion, she slept.

LA schools were different. Teachers had resources and patience. Nilima had no detentions in six months, no punishments for being herself. She admired her math teacher, Ms. Seefried, who captivated her with her commitment, comparing her to the saying, "The angels are not on my shoulder—they are among us." Nilima's mother often said that a human is "manhush," a famous Bengali word that combines "man," meaning value, and "hush," meaning awareness. Ms. Seefried embodied the true meaning of being "manhush."

She loved living with her uncle's family. She discovered different talents she hadn't known about, such as winning a handwriting contest and writing a detailed essay that moved her teacher. Being in LA made her feel liberated from bigotry. The apartment complex sat atop a hill; she enjoyed the daily walk down to the bus, surrounded by trees and sunlight. Although she had made no friends yet, she felt at peace, appreciating her own company and the nature around her.

Every Saturday brought tension between her parents as they discussed whether to stay or return. Ultimately, her father announced he was moving to NYC, while they stayed behind until he found an apartment.

Although the news was sudden, Nilima realized that LA had been too good to last.

She discussed her feelings with her teachers, who encouraged her to remain optimistic. The resource teachers invited Nilima and Paul, a Vietnamese classmate, to dinner for winning the handwriting and essay contest. Nilima wore her best thrift-store dress, a green, knee-length dress that had white borders. The teachers picked her up from the apartment.

As she went inside the car, she saw another boy in the back seat. She knew him, Paul; they had class together. Paul said, "Hi, how are you?" Nilima replied, "I am good. Glad you came," Paul talked a lot; Nilima thought, he spoke about what he learned at school, what he wants to do in the future, and how much he likes the teachers.

Nilima rolled her eyes and looked outside the window. The teacher asked if they liked the Japanese Restaurant. Nilima replied, "I never had Japanese food," and Paul nodded in response.

As they entered the restaurant, the waiter greeted them and said, "Your table is ready under Judy." They sat at the table, Paul and Nilima on one side, and the teachers on the other. They conversed about how proud they were of them for coming to a new country, learning a new culture and language, yet still doing so well in school.

Nilima wasn't sure if she was hearing right. She thought, "Me? Doing well?" One of the teachers asked, "Nilima, what do you want to be when you grow up?" She paused for a moment and replied, "I want to work somewhere where I will be traveling the whole world."

Nilima explained that she has always wondered about different climates and countries, and that she knows about them only through books. She wants to know about other cultures; she wants to live with other people to learn about their daily habits and customs, such as what they eat and do. The teacher listened enthusiastically and encouraged Nilima to work toward her goal. She had a wonderful time; she never felt so at ease.

When she came home, everyone was inquisitive about the evening. Nilima didn't say much; she doesn't like to be the center of attention. She slept well that night. The evening was joyful, filled with curiosity about food, culture, and future dreams. Her teachers' encouragement left her feeling understood, seen, and valued.

A few weeks later, Nilima encountered something she never expected would happen in the best country in the world. The thought that LA was safe and everyone is seen as the same was dissipated when the social studies teacher opened the discussion on race in America.

She was a young teacher, a recent graduate, with light brown, curly hair, about 5 feet 5 inches, thin, and having greenish-blue eyes. She was wearing a dress that came to her shin and a pair of black sandals, with her hair pulled back and pinned.

The teacher announced that an incident occurred a few days ago involving a black man who was brutally killed for speeding. The 1992 Los Angeles riots were a significant event in American history, sparked by the acquittal of four LAPD officers who had been videotaped beating Rodney King, an African American motorist, during a traffic stop in March 1991.

Nilima didn't understand the whole concept. Seconds later, she realized the teacher was talking about the racial tension in America. "Race was never an issue in Bangladesh," she spoke out, "Because everyone is the same". Nilima then realized it is not true at all; the color of skin is a big issue in South Asia, too.

Girls with darker skin get married later and are not considered pretty. She raised her hand and told the class that even in South Asia, where everyone is the same, the shade of brown mattered. The class listened, and then the teacher asked a question that made Nilima think deeply.

The teacher asked, "Why is it that the darker skin is considered a lower status? Why do you think, after so many years of freedom, racial tension still exists? What are your thoughts on racial struggle in America?"

That was the homework. Nilima thought about it all day but didn't know why people think the way they think. All she knew was that people's skin color only depends on where their ancestors lived.

Places where the weather is warmer tend to have people with darker skin, and vice versa. Nilima stopped writing and thought beyond that; it's just people's feelings toward one another. How do we address that? How can we learn that everyone is good and bad, regardless of the color of their skin?

She could not finish her assignment because she genuinely didn't have an answer. To her, only what you do mattered, only what is seen in action mattered. Good actions are the universal truth, and everything else is just not necessary, like how we look, short or tall, fair or dark, rich or poor, nothing matters.

She didn't know why racial tension existed, and similarly, she didn't understand the civil rights movement. Making her feel out of place, perhaps it's not reality, perhaps it is the hell everyone talks about.

Whatever it is, her thought about race is that maybe different cultures made it very hard to blend in, and everyone thinks their own culture and race is better than others. She felt distraught that she could not explain or answer the questions properly. She thought about it all night and was convinced that she could explain it better in class. She slept with her assignment lying next to her.

Little did she know that the assignment would never be submitted, and she would never have the opportunity to discuss her idea. In the morning, all the schools were closed because of the safety of students, as protests and violence spread throughout LA. Nilima was spellbound that something like this would happen. This racial struggle is bigger than she imagined, much more complicated than she realized, and maybe it will be a never-ending struggle.

Finally, the day came to reunite with her father in NYC. At the same time, the Breakfast at her uncle's house was interrupted by a tremor—the earthquake in Big Bear Lake, California. Nilima instinctively ducked under the table with her brother, recalling school drills. When it ended, news confirmed a 6.5-magnitude quake, felt across LA and the suburbs. Her mother, anxious about their flight, tried to stay calm.

Over the last two years, mother had grown close to her toddler cousin, Omar, who called her "Jelly" and clung to her every night. Saying goodbye at the airport was heart-wrenching, and she marveled at the depth of such selfless love.

The flight to NYC was quiet and reflective. Fourteen-year-old Nilima, with short, carefree hair, watched dense city lights from the airplane window, pondering her new life. The "city that never sleeps" felt strange, overwhelming, and unfamiliar. The taxi ride to their new redbrick apartment offered no comfort. The narrow hallways, flickering lights, and a small basement unit were all too overwhelming—but the smell of curry and jasmine rice reminded her of home.

Dinner was simple. Her father confessed their financial limits, yet her mother smiled, finding blessings in the smallest things. That night, Nilima lay on the floor with her siblings, diary in hand, contemplating her place in NYC. Excitement and apprehension mingled together. Perhaps I don't want to be part of this play. Perhaps my role is not the one I want. Life is a story without a clear destination. Exhausted, she fell asleep, wondering how her siblings felt about it all.

Florida January 2021

The Last Plea

She was back in her apartment, sitting at the dining table. She loses time and memories of her last whereabouts. It's been a while since she had an episode. The tiny apartment was so quiet, yet the humming of the air conditioner, the leaky faucet, and the neighbor's footsteps upstairs seemed so loud. The apartment was modestly furnished with a small, rounded table and chairs, a narrow bed pushed against the wall, and a side table displaying a few books. A single lamp in the corner of the room adds just a faint glow across the room.

As she stood by the window, there were no curtains to soften the streetlight or shield her from the outside world. The glass on the window sometimes reflected some of the people who died holding her hand. She thought about how profoundly people can touch her heart, some to help her be better, and others to act as teachers guiding her along.

She would place a stone in a jar for each patient she assisted in death. As she looked at the jar, it was filling up, and she could recall many faces of death, nor the name, but she could not forget the experience of being present. As her unit became a COVID-Tier II ICU, she was also trained rapidly to become a skilled nurse. Nilima experienced unanticipated deaths followed by either code blue or intubation.

Many patients gave consent to intubate, knowing that they might not make it…Yet the last plea to live. Once Nilima gets consent, the patient is prepared for intubation, and the ICU doctor is notified.

About two weeks ago, Nilima saw a *man-hush* encountering an intubation event that took place with a patient. Nilima had witnessed many emergencies in her years of practice, but something about that day pressed more deeply into her consciousness. She had seen people gasp, panic, plead, or fade quietly—yet the moment she watched unfold felt like a hush settling over the world, as though time itself had bowed its head in respect for what was happening.

It was not the intubation itself that struck her; she had seen that procedure countless times. It was the stillness in the room, the almost sacred pause before the chaos of intervention. The patient lay vulnerable, suspended between breath and no breath, life and something beyond it. The air felt thick, almost reverent, as if the walls understood the gravity of what the medical team was about to do.

The on-call ICU physician that day stepped forward with his usual quietness. He was known for his humility—rare in a space where authorities often walked with rigid shoulders and clipped words. He was a man who could balance clinical precision with an astonishing ability to keep his humanity intact. Unlike many, he did not fuse his identity with outcomes; he knew that medicine was not omnipotent, that not every act of care would bend fate.

Nilima always admired that about him. He never allowed the cold calculations of treatment protocols to overshadow the warmth of human presence. He knew the science, yes—but he also knew the limits of it. He recognized that even when every step was executed perfectly, the universe might still refuse to cooperate. And yet, he came back each day, steady and unbroken, like someone who had made peace with the duality of his role: healer and witness, controller and powerless observer.

That day, the ICU hummed with a steady, artificial life—machines breathing, monitors chirping, fluorescent lights buzzing faintly overhead. The air was cool, almost cold, carrying the sterile scent of alcohol wipes, plastic tubing, and the faint metallic smell of oxygen. Every sound echoed slightly, as though the room itself was holding its breath.

She prepared for the intubation in quiet concentration—laryngoscope blades laid out, IV syringes prefilled with sedatives, suction checked and ready. Each action was deliberate, mechanical, yet she felt a tremor of unease, as if the walls themselves sensed what was coming.

Behind her, soft but unsteady footsteps approached. The ICU physician stopped just outside the doorway, rooted in the border between the hallway's brightness and the dim patient room. His posture sagged, shoulders folded inward.

He stepped out of the room and rested against the wall. He removed the face shield and his glasses, revealing eyes of worry, exhaustion, and grief. Slowly, he took off the N95 mask, the gloves, and his own glasses. And then, without warning, he broke.

His breath faltered. Tears welled, then spilled freely, tracking down his face in trembling lines.

"I feel like a failure," he whispered, voice raw and cracking. "This will be the fifth patient I'm intubating… and I know he's going to die. We're extubating early because of shortages, and there's nothing I can do to stop it."

The truth hung heavily between them. She watched him—this man who usually carried crisis with stoic resolve—now unraveling in the hallway, vulnerable in a way she had never seen.

Around them, the ICU continued its relentless rhythm: alarms, footsteps, hushed murmurs, ventilators cycling. But in that narrow strip of space, it felt like the world had narrowed to just two people and an impossible moral weight.

He wiped his eyes with shaking hands and forced himself to breathe deeply. Slowly, he rebuilt his armor—mask repositioned, gown retied, glasses set back onto the bridge of his nose. His hands still trembled as he stepped into the room.

Inside, she administered the etomidate, ketamine, and propofol. The respiratory therapist (RT) stood ready at the head of the bed, ventilator tubing in hand.

The doctor lifted the laryngoscope. His fingers trembled visibly.

"Alright… let's do this," he murmured, though the words sounded more like he was trying to convince himself.

He inserted the blade—but the angle wasn't right. The patient's anatomy was difficult, and the doctor's grip was unsteady. His hand shook, the light beam wavering. The ET tube scraped against the back of the throat, but not the cords.

"Doctor…" the RT said softly but firmly, watching the monitor. "Sat's dropping. Ninety-one… eighty-nine."

"I see it," the doctor muttered, voice tight. His breathing quickened. He adjusted his grip, but his hand tremored again.

The RT stepped closer. "Pull out. Pull out. Let's bag again."

The doctor hesitated, panic flickering in his eyes. "I can get it—"

"Doc," the RT said, gentler now but unwavering, "his sat is eighty-five. Pull out. We'll reoxygenate."

The doctor froze, blade still in hand, then slowly withdrew. His hands shook so badly that he almost dropped the laryngoscope. The RT immediately applied the bag-valve mask and began ventilating in steady, practiced squeezes.

"Okay, we're going back up—eighty-eight… ninety-two… ninety-six," the RT announced, eyes on the monitor.

The doctor stepped back, swallowing hard. Sweat beaded at his temples. His hands trembled uncontrollably. He stared at them, horrified.

"I—I've never…" He inhaled sharply. "My hands… I can't stop shaking."

The RT met his eyes—not with judgment, but understanding. "It's okay. Happens to everyone eventually. This job… it takes from you." He paused, voice softening. "You're not failing. You're trying under impossible conditions."

The doctor pressed a hand against the counter to steady himself. "I can't lose another one," he whispered.

The RT placed a gentle hand on the doctor's shoulder. "We're gonna do it together. Second pass. Slow. Steady. I've got your back."

After a few grounding breaths, the doctor nodded, regaining a fraction of control. "Okay. Second attempt."

When he lifted the blade again, his hand still trembled—but the RT braced the patient's jaw, guiding him, anchoring him. The team leaned in, silent, united in the effort.

This time, the cords came into view.

This time, the tube slid through.

This time, a faint sigh of relief passed through the room.

As the ventilator engaged with its steady whoosh-whoosh rhythm, the moral weight returned—unchanged but shared. The doctor stood still for several moments, staring at the ventilator screen with haunted eyes.

Saving a life had never felt so close to losing one. One week later, that patient dies.

Core Humanism

Nilima returns to the same lockdown unit, and the moment the room seemed to hold its breath as an intubation unfolded under the hum of fluorescent lights and the steady pulse of monitors. What struck her was not just the clinical gravity but the moral landscape that revealed itself in the quiet gestures, the trembling hands, and the unspoken truths that lived behind every decision.

The ongoing influx of COVID patients helped Nilima transform internally. Looking beyond the flesh and bone and beyond the self. As she prepares the medications, takes the report, talks to the family for an update, and cares for patients, she feels the unshakeable stillness that comes before every death. The room seemed to acknowledge the gravity of the act: one breath being surrendered to a machine, one life suspended between the known and the uncertain.

Standing by the window at her apartment, she remembered the many older patients who had refused intubation during those overwhelming days. Their reasoning was never rooted in fear. If anything, it was rooted in love.

"I've had my time," one elderly man had whispered, voice raspy but firm. "Save the ventilators for someone younger."

Another woman, her hands trembling as she signed the DNR form, had said, "Let the young people breathe. I want my grandchildren to see tomorrow."

These were not passive resignations; they were moral acts. Selfless acts. Decisions shaped by a profound sense of justice—the ethical principle that resources should be used fairly, that care must be distributed with equity, not emotion. Their refusals echoed the belief that fairness sometimes meant stepping aside so that another life might have a chance.

And then there was beneficence—the duty to do good, to act in the patient's best interest. Nilima had always understood beneficence as a guiding star of nursing, but in those moments, she realized its complexity. Doing good was not always the same as prolonging life. Sometimes, beneficence meant honoring a patient's wish not to suffer. Sometimes it meant accepting that the kindest care was allowing nature to take its course.

As the physician lifted the laryngoscope, his hands trembled—not from inexperience, but from the weight of these moral realities. Behind his face shield, his eyes carried the exhaustion of someone who had spent too many nights choosing which patients to intubate and which to ease into comfort care. The principle of justice had become heartbreakingly tangible in those days of scarcity. Every tube, every ventilator, represented a decision that rippled far beyond the patient in front of them.

Healthcare humility, steady acceptance of responsibility, reminded her of why she had become a nurse in the first place: not to cure, not to fix, but to serve.

At graduation, we were asked to recite:

"To serve ethically.

To serve compassionately.

To serve with a conscience."

Nilima had thought it a bit ceremonial, even silly—never fully grasping the weight of those words. Yet, as time passed, she realized how experience transforms that backdrop of noise into the quiet, guiding rhythm of growth.

And now in this dim room, surrounded by the mechanical whisper of the ventilator and the quiet concentration of the team, she felt something shift inside her. Nursing was not merely a series of tasks or competencies; it was a moral practice. A discipline of the mind and the heart.

She understood now that *beneficence* was not a gentle idea—it was an active commitment to do what is right, even when right is difficult. *Justice* was not an abstract principle—it was a lived reality in every allocation of resources, every conversation about prognosis, every whispered refusal from an elderly patient choosing dignity over intervention.

The true ethics of nursing were not found in textbooks, she realized, but in the silent moments where life and choice intersected. In honoring the autonomy of those who declined treatment. In advocating for fairness in times of scarcity. In witnessing suffering without turning away. In carrying the memories of patients whose decisions had quietly shaped the lives of others.

Every day, the COVID unit became more than a clinical space. It became a classroom of humanity, where every breath, every silence, every decision revealed a more profound truth about what it meant to care.

And as Nilima stepped back from the bedside, listening to the ventilator's rhythmic sigh, she felt a renewed sense of purpose—steady, ethical, unwavering.

A commitment to serve not only with knowledge, but with justice.

Not only with skill, but with beneficence.

Not only in healing—

But in honoring the profound, fragile humanity at the center of every choice.

Nilima came to understand that the nursing ethics taught in classrooms—beneficence, justice, fidelity—were not abstract principles to memorize. They were already embedded in the human spirit. Her patients had shown her that beneath fear, suffering, and uncertainty lived a profound capacity to love, to sacrifice, and to accept—even for strangers they would never truly know. Their choices, their strength, and their quiet dignity left her with a heavy heart, not from sorrow alone, but from the overwhelming realization of what human beings are capable of at the edge of life's most difficult moments.

Presence

One day, she returned to the COVID unit and was assigned to be a mentor. The orientee was twenty-four, bright-eyed, eager, and untested in the face of mortality. She had spent a year in a medical-surgical telemetry unit, where monitors beeped, and medications flowed, but death had always remained distant, almost abstract. Her name is Jennifer. Now she stood on the COVID floor, confronted with patients whose fragility was relentless. She had joined this floor to advance her career, unaware that the experience awaiting her would reshape not only her skills, but her understanding of life itself.

Nilima sensed the weight of what lay ahead. This would not be a simple teaching moment. It would be a moral, emotional, and human lesson that the orientee would never forget. Nilima needed to remain steady—for the patient. We recently received approval to use Zoom to communicate with family members and show the patient. Nilima needs to be resilient not only for the family watching through Zoom, but also for the young nurse learning beside her. Yet inside, she carried a storm of emotion, a deep ache she could not expel.

Yet another patient declined intubation but wanted to eat his favorite food before he died. It began with something seemingly ordinary—a bite of soup. He wanted the soup his wife makes when he is sick at home. As he took the first bite, the patient began to cough violently, food entering the lungs. Oxygen saturation dropped; alarms screamed, and the heart rate surged. Nilima acted instinctively: she removed the food, raised the head of the bed, and guided the patient forward, letting him continue to cough while she explained the reasoning to the family.

"I think it's wise to start giving him morphine for comfort, so he can relax," Nilima said softly.

"Please make him comfortable. He is hurting," the wife responded, tears streaming down her face.

Nilima nodded and explained, "We will give morphine every fifteen minutes. It will make him lethargic, and eventually, he will fall asleep peacefully. His heart will continue for a while, but he won't feel the pain anymore. This is the kindest thing we can do for him now."

The next thirty minutes stretched like decades. Every heartbeat, every sigh, every alarm carried the weight of mortality. Nilima sat beside the patient, removed her gloves, and held his hand, whispering calm comfort. Jennifer assisted with the last doses, her eyes wide with both fear and awe. And then—the monitor flattened. Breathing ceased. Pulse became absent. Nilima confirmed the time of death and documented it, her hand still resting gently on the patient's chest.

In all this rushed moment, Nilima was still, looking at the orientee. The young nurse was so devastated that she felt agonizing pain. She was hyperventilating, tears were streaming down partly making the N95 wet, and the face shield was foggy as she kept wiping it off with her gloved hands.

When the family requested that the Zoom be turned off, the room fell silent. Nilima turned to the orientee, noticing the weight of the moment reflected in her expression—shock, awe, and a dawning comprehension.

"Nilima… I… I've never seen anyone die before," the young nurse said softly. Her voice trembled. "I thought I was ready for critical care, but… this is so different. I don't know if I can ever… handle this."

Nilima placed a steady hand on her shoulder. "It's okay to feel that way. You can step out if you want to get fresh air."

"No, I want to stay with you," Jannifer replied.

Nilima thought to herself, *I wish you didn't come to COVID just yet. So young with so much death will leave a lasting impact on their mental health.*

But Nilima did not say anything.

The orientee looked down, swallowing hard. "I joined this floor to advance my career… to learn, to become better, to maybe one day lead. I didn't think… I didn't realize I'd be learning about life itself. It feels overwhelming."

Nilima nodded, her eyes soft. "COVID is different; it's not regular nursing. You'll learn about monitors, medications, procedures—but more importantly, you'll learn about humanity. About dignity, about suffering, about the weight of choices we make. Every patient here teaches you something about life, about death, and about the responsibility we carry as nurses."

Jannifer hesitated, then whispered, "I want to help people… really help. But how do I stay strong when everything feels like it's breaking me?"

Nilima smiled gently. "You don't have to be unbreakable. Strength is not the absence of emotion—it's holding your compassion alongside your action. It's being present, even when it hurts. And sometimes, it's knowing that helping someone means guiding them to peace, not only prolonging life. That's what we do here. That's humanism. That's nursing."

The young nurse looked up, eyes glimmering with tears, now gasping.

"Yes," Nilima replied. "Freedom. Liberation. The patient is free from suffering now. And you—learning this lesson, being present—you're free too, from the illusion that we can control everything. You'll carry this lesson with you your whole life. That's what it means to witness with humanity."

They returned their attention to the quiet monitor, to the empty rhythms of the room. Nilima reflected again on the patients who had refused intervention for the sake of others, who had chosen to step aside so younger generations might live.

"You'll remember this moment," Nilima said softly, squeezing the orientee's hand. "Not because it was easy, but because it matters. Nursing is about presence, about moral courage, and about love—sometimes in ways you can't measure. That's the real education. That's the education that stays with you."

Jennifer nodded, silent now, absorbing the enormity of what she had witnessed. In the rushed COVID unit, surrounded by monitors and machines, she understood for the first time that life and death are inseparable, and that every compassionate act—every handheld, every gentle word—carries its own liberation.

Nilima was breaking inside, but didn't realize that she said all that.

Nilima, watching the young nurse and herself take the first steps toward understanding the sacred weight of nursing, realized again that this was why she had chosen this path: to witness, to guide, and to serve humanity, one fleeting, fragile life at a time.

Coming out of the room, the new nurse hugged her as she broke down in tears, saying, "He could not even eat his soup." It was her very first death, very first day as a nurse on the COVID unit. Nilima froze as she too could not hold her tears. She felt defeated each time, fighting a war.

Suddenly…she felt out of place…she was dizzy…confused

Why is she experiencing the shift of time again??? She tried to shake off her thoughts…she muttered, "This is not the time or place." She rushed to the restroom and washed her face. Things seemed to be settling down…she went back to the unit.

In those final hours of life, while sitting close to the patients, she saw the dance of the fragile beauty of life, both at its triumph and regret. Between the conversation and the humming of the machine, she remembered the spoken love, the cherished ones, the dreams they pursue, and the feeling of abandonment.

Between the rounds of IV morphine injection and Scopolamine to maintain oral secretion, the death of each patient was unique. Some died with one round of morphine, and some died after 45 minutes of agonal breathing and discomfort. She often took her gloves off during their last breath, holding hands skin to skin, being the only person of comfort. Every single patient left something in her, a composition of different emotions, gratitude, connectedness, or a sense of longing.

Throughout the orientation with Jennifer, Nilima saw how she became a confident nurse, a transformed nurse with so much grace and compassion. This profession can change you to be better or worse out of frustration and stress.

At the apartment, there was loneliness surrounding her, a compassionate one that ached in the hollow of her chest, but somehow that gave her an unfamiliar calmness. A life of solitude demands so much less from life, stripped and raw, nothing she had ever understood before.

The loneliness is not entirely empty; it is filled with stories of love and loss, unfulfilled wishes, and acceptance with gratitude when time is near.

The last breath may be gone; the words are saved with their loved one's heart like embers that glow. The deaths she encountered were not the end or silence, but instead echoes of love and teaching that life offers, reminding us that change is a constant.

The daily death of patients in the COVID unit brought a different perspective to her life, she thought as she prepared for another day of triumph… trying to sleep…then it happens again.

NYC High School 1993- 1996

Unspoken

Nilima didn't know how she felt about her high school in New York City. The streets of Astoria, Queens, weren't her favorite; she missed the suburbs of Los Angeles. She missed the perfect weather, the hilly roads, and the cedar and magnolia trees that perfumed her evening walks to her uncle's house. In Astoria, the sidewalks were bare, the plants planted ten feet apart looked staged, and her daily walk to the subway with her sister felt like a chore. Her father had taught them how to ride the subway the summer before school started. The subway was exciting at first, but eventually, she felt as if she were in a laboratory maze—always running in circles, never belonging.

High school was a blur of identity crisis, adaptation, and searching for meaning—until junior year. That year, Nilima found a few close friends: Michelle, Lolita, and Jennifer. "No judgments, no boundaries," Jennifer had told her once as they sat at lunch, laughing at some inside joke. Nilima felt safe with them, as if spring had finally bloomed in her life.

But the real turning point was English class. That was when she first noticed Eric. He wasn't a popular kid; he kept to himself mostly, but when he read or when the teacher recited his work, something about his words struck her soul.

"Eric, would you mind sharing what you wrote?" the teacher would ask.

Eric would sigh dramatically, flip his paper, and begin to read aloud. Nilima sat silently, memorizing every phrase. Later, she'd scribble the lines in her notebook. At night, she'd whisper them to herself. How can someone write so beautifully? she wondered. She wasn't in love with how he looked, but with his mind, his words, his voice.

By senior year, they shared more classes, including physics. Physics was her downfall. Every time the teacher called her to the board, she froze. One afternoon, after class, Eric leaned toward her desk.

"I can help you with physics, you know," he said casually.

Nilima's throat tightened. She couldn't make eye contact. "That… that would be nice of you," she managed.

So, they began meeting fifteen minutes before school to work on homework. Truthfully, Nilima rarely ever remembered much of what he explained; she only remembered his voice. Sometimes, when he spoke, she would stare at the curve of his mouth and think of the way his essays made her feel.

"Can I read your latest poem?" she asked one morning.

He grinned. "Sure. I'll make you a copy. But you're the only one I'll trust with it."

Those poems became her treasures, kept neatly in a folder. She read them repeatedly, memorizing his words as if they belonged to her.

Graduation came too quickly. Nilima had planned to finally tell him everything—to confess her feelings, to get his number before he left for college in Pennsylvania. After the ceremony, he rushed up to her, excitement in his eyes.

"Nilima! Come with me, I want you to meet someone!"

Her heart leaped. He wants me to meet his parents, she thought, her palms sweaty. She laughed nervously, "Wow, it's hot today," as she took off her gown.

But then she saw the girl. Curly brown hair, glasses, a soft smile.

"This is Lisa, my girlfriend," Eric said proudly. "She went to Catholic school, but she lives next door to me."

Nilima's vision blurred. She forced a smile and hugged Lisa. "Hi, it's so nice to meet you. You two make such a beautiful couple."

Lisa smiled warmly. "Eric doesn't stop talking about you, Nilima. He says you're such a good friend."

Nilima's stomach dropped, but she steadied her voice. "That's sweet of him."

When Eric asked for her number, she scribbled it down quickly—except it wasn't her real number. As she walked away, she whispered to herself, *Stop shaking. Stop crying. Don't you dare break now.*

On the subway ride home, her mother noticed her silence. "Tor ki holo? Ato chup keno, keno eto sad?" (What is with the silence? Why are you so sad?)

Nilima bit her lip hard, willing herself not to scream. Later that night, she took out her treasured folder, reread his essays and poems once more, then tore them into pieces. The sound of the paper ripping was similar to the sound of her heart breaking.

The next morning, she cried in the shower, her sobs drowned by the running water. Summer came, and Eric was gone. She missed his voice, his laugh, and the way he made physics seem less terrifying and poetry more alive.

She had known him since the first day of high school, when he'd directed her to the right classroom. Now, his absence echoed through every book she picked up, every memory she tried to bury.

She missed him, his voice, and how his laugh echoed when she tried to read a book. They talked about so many topics, from physics to theater to music to human emotions. Nilima had never found anyone like him.

Three years had passed by, and Nilima was now in her third year of college. She had grown into a thin, tall woman, her hair long and full, and her walk more graceful than she realized. Sometimes, her friends teased her.

"Nilima, why are you torturing yourself with computer programming?" one friend joked over coffee in the cafeteria. "You should just be a model. You'd make more money and have more fun."

Nilima rolled her eyes, flicking her pen against her notebook.

"Oh, please," she replied with a small laugh. "Modeling? I can barely stand still for a picture without blinking. Besides, I like solving problems—even if they take me forever."

Her friends giggled, shaking their heads, but Nilima smiled faintly. Behind the laughter, her heart still carried the weight of Eric's absence—the boy whose words once lit up her world. His voice had faded into memory, and though she told herself she was fine, she often wondered if she'd ever feel that way again.

At home, her parents had a different concern. Every evening, the same conversations echoed around the dinner table.

"Nilima, you're old enough," her mother said one night, her voice gentle but persistent. "We've even seen some good men. You can't study books forever."

Her father added firmly, "Marriage gives stability. You'll understand once you settle down. Life isn't just about degrees and friends."

Nilima stared at her plate, pushing the rice with her fork. "I don't know if I'm ready," she whispered.

Her parents brought a few "eligible" grooms for her, but something always goes wrong. Nilima doesn't wear the Indian outfit or have makeup on. One time, she came out with sweat pants and a t-shirt on and looked at the groom in the eyes and said, "What's up, dude?" while chewing gum. The guy left so fast that he forgot to take his belongings with him.

But after months of persuasion, she agreed to meet someone. She just wanted to leave the house. She thought that would be a way to break free from where she does not belong.

The man her parents chose was polite, respectful, with a stable career and a calm smile. He asked her questions, complimented her hair, and spoke about his plans for the future. Nilima listened quietly, her heart still, like a sea waiting for waves.

Later that night, standing in her room, she whispered to herself in the mirror:

My heart is like an ocean... wide, endless. I can accept anyone. I can learn to love anyone. Right?

And so, she married him….

But from the very first day, an ache began to grow. She tried to smile through it, to be the dutiful wife, the obedient daughter, but something inside her resisted. The walls of the house felt too small, the expectations too heavy.

One evening, 16 years later, she met an old college friend for tea. They embraced each other warmly, but as her friend stepped back, she studied Nilima's face with concern.

"What happened to you?" the friend asked softly. "The bubbly Nilima I knew—the one who laughed at everything, joked around, and dreamed of possibilities—she's gone. Now I just see a woman… carrying sadness."

Nilima forced a laugh, but her throat tightened. "Oh, I guess that's what marriage does. Life changes us."

Her friend shook her head, almost in disbelief. "No, Nilima. Life doesn't kill joy. Something else did."

Nilima looked down at her teacup, the steam rising like unspoken words. She wanted to scream and to tell her friend about the emptiness, the way she never truly belonged in this minuscule concept of life—this cage of expectation.

But she whispered, "I don't know where I stand anymore."

And in her silence, the ocean inside her remained restless, its waves crashing against unseen shores.

Florida Sept 2021

The Enigma Of Belonging

The park was empty, surrounded by silence except for the restless wind. She sat alone on a weathered bench beneath the wide canopy of a weeping willow. The branches hung low, like arms reaching out to console her. Her body shook with sobs, but the tree seemed to answer—its leaves rustling gently, almost as if nature itself was sharing her sorrow.

For seven years, she had been visiting this tree. It had seen her laughter, her quiet walks, her scattered thoughts, and now her grief. She followed it through the seasons, and somehow, in its enduring presence, she had found security. Today, however, the comfort felt fragile.

Eventually, she rose and strolled back towards her car. Each step felt heavy, weighted with questions she had carried for years. People, she thought, are made to belong. To love, to be loved in return, to weave themselves into the fabric of another's life. Why was it denied to her? She had lived long enough to know that love does not vanish, even when it has no place to take root. The energy of it survives, changing its shape, but never dying. It lingers in memory, in desire, in the marrow of one's being. It is an enigma—beautiful and cruel.

Her hand touched the car door handle. She sat, and started the car…and just then, a melody rose from the radio. A Bengali song. Her breath caught.

Jibano maroner simana chhaaraye,

Bondhu hey aamar, royechho dnaanray…

The voice carried through the twilight air, carrying the weight of home, of childhood, and of something sacred she had never fully embraced until later in life. She whispered to herself the English she once translated:

Beyond the arena of life and death,

O, my friend, you remain standing.

Within the deserted horizon of my heart,

Brightly shining is your throne so great…

Tears welled up again. How strange it was that the older she became, the more fiercely she longed to know her culture. In her early thirties, she had begun retracing the Bengali alphabet, and slowly, as though returning to a language she had abandoned but never truly lost. She was fluent in speech—her tongue carried conversations efficiently—but the literature demanded more: patience, discipline, and reverence.

Through this re-learning, she encountered Tagore. She had grown up hearing his songs, along with the Nazrul fiery verses, which drifted through her parents' home in Bangladesh and later in their small apartment in New York. But only now, in her forties, did the words strike her with full force.

At forty-one, Tagore ceased to be merely a poet; he became her companion, her guide, her rescuer. The broken ruins of her failed twenty-year marriage couldn't consume her because she was consumed by something larger—his words, his music, his philosophy, and the sanctuary she found in the natural world.

Nature became her scripture. She saw its hidden rhythms everywhere. The waves rushing to shore—rising, falling, pausing. Each movement had its measure, its interval of silence. There was equilibrium in the space between a crest crashing against the sand and the next wave forming out at sea. She listened to the wind stirring the willow leaves; even that had rhythm, a breath that rose and fell.

Nature was music, and music was nature. Together, they served as her refuge. They taught her balance, offered her meaning when the human world gave none.

But today, all of it slipped through her fingers. Why now, she wondered, did her past come surging back like a flood? Why this sudden breaking? Was this her true self unraveling? Or had she been unraveling all along without noticing it?

Alone in the parking lot, she pressed her forehead against the car window. Loneliness was no longer a passing ache; it was a force pressing into her bones.

Later, in the hollow quiet of her apartment, she collapsed onto her bed. Thoughts circled endlessly. She had always been alone, even among friends, family, and colleagues. Different. Awkward. Misplaced. She had never fit into any mold. Not fully Bangladeshi, not fully Indian, not fully American. She belonged to no land, no culture, no nation.

What was she, then, but a mere existence? A figure moving through time unnoticed. A life so trivial that her absence would ripple no further than the vanishing form of a broken wave. Life would continue, the rivers would flow, the sun would rise, the tides would turn—whether or not she existed at all.

At last, her tears stilled. Exhaustion claimed her.

And as she drifted into sleep, she felt herself slipping away—not into oblivion, but into something else. Another time. Another realm. Something beyond the reach of this lonely night.

British India 1910

The Forest Of Betrayal

Nilima walked into her house, not making any eye contact with anyone. She gathered a few clothes, a necklace her mother had given her, and a notebook of her poems, in which she writes poems in her free time. She didn't pack anything else.

Nilima was twenty years old. She went to a forest and seemed to be waiting for someone, and the year was 1910!!!

In the 1910s, these woodlands were vast—like living cathedrals—resonant with hums, fragrances, and colors so alive they seemed to breathe. The towering sal, teak, and bamboo groves stretched toward the sky, filtering sunlight that danced restlessly across the forest floor.

She felt enveloped by the flames of the Glory Lily, the golden blaze of the Palash, and the intoxicating fragrance of Kanak-chopa flowers. She had never experienced nature like this—not in memory, not in dream, not in any form of consciousness. Looking down, she saw the ground carpeted with moss, ferns, and fallen leaves, forming a natural tapestry beneath her feet. In the distance, monkeys leaped from tree to tree, a chorus of parakeets shattered the silence, and butterflies drifted lazily around her. In that moment, Nilima felt the coexistence of life—trees, birds, animals, and herself—as one belonging, one harmony.

20-year-old Nilima looked serene, almost tranquil, yet her heart trembled with worry as she strolled slowly, her saree rustling softly with each step. She was draped in the traditional Bengali attire of her time: a saree pleats tightly tucked at her waist, the pallu falling in folds over her shoulders. A small golden nose ring glinted against her skin, bangles—too large for her slender wrists—clinked as she moved, and anklets jingled with each step. Her long, thick braid was decorated with flowers, swaying gently behind her.

Nilima paused by the trunk of a teak tree, resting against it as her fingers idly traced the grooves of its bark. Then she saw him. A figure moving toward her, a young man also in his twenties. Her arms relaxed, and her eyes lit up with unspoken joy.

He approached silently at first, simply observing her, as though memorizing her presence. When he got close enough, he brushed her hair back and gently touched her cheek. She lifted her gaze to his face, and in that instant, she knew—his presence would devastate her.

Pulling slightly away, she steadied herself. His voice came soft, almost breaking:

"You mean a lot to me, Nilima. But this Hindu–Muslim conflict will keep us apart. I am sorry."

Her eyes widened in disbelief. She argued—what about our love, about its power, and its purity. But he only shook his head, his voice tender and resolute.

"Love does not always mean togetherness. Sometimes it means loving from afar."

Her heart swelled, defiant. "The only true love is unconditional love, one that demands sacrifice, commitment, and the courage to fight for justice. Will you fight—for us?"

He lowered his gaze. "I am sorry," he whispered again, taking her hand in his own for the last time.

Her voice broke as she begged: "Then marry me in the next life?"

He gave a faint, sorrowful smile. "We have only this one life, Nilima. But in it, I will always cherish you."

He continued, "And if the teaching of my father is true, I will marry you in the next life if you have the right religion, right caste, and right status". He smiled with sorrow because he knew he was defeated. He knows he gave up on love.

And with that, he turned away. Slowly, his figure faded into the depths of the forest, each step dissolving like smoke into the air, until only distance and silence remained. Nilima stood rooted, her urge to run after him crushed by the weight of inevitability. The force of her emotions gradually ebbed, leaving her hollow.

At last, she sank beneath the shade of the teak tree, lifeless, listening to the forest breathe around her. The cathedral of trees that once embraced her now echoed with loss. She felt so insignificant, smaller than a grain of sand.

British India

The Uninvited Union

It all started at a Durga Puja celebration, which is filled with color, music, and food. Nilima met him at his courtyard. His family is a wealthy Brahmin family and invites the whole town to celebrate with them. He is happy to receive the paise because he is the only wealthy Brahmin who accepts everyone, regardless of caste, creed, or religion. He not only invites all castes and religions, but also truly entertains them equally. Lanterns swung from the trees, casting a golden light across the courtyard. Families gathered in their finest attire, children ran barefoot, and the air smelled of spices, sweets, and incense.

Nilima moved with her natural grace through the crowd, her laughter light and unrestrained, greeting everyone with warmth. She developed so much respect knowing their openness about humanity.

It was there, amid the chaos and joy, that she saw him, his posture simple yet confident, eyes clear and observant. Their worlds, seemingly so separate and different, collided in a moment of accidental proximity.

He noticed her first—the way she laughed without reservation, the way her eyes softened when she spoke to children and elders alike. There was a rare freedom about her, an effortless kindness. She, in turn, admired him—the calm authenticity in his movements, the simplicity with which he navigated the crowd, the gentleness in his gaze that seemed to see people for who they truly were.

He came up to her and introduced himself, "Hi, my name is Ravi." That night, they talked endlessly, drenched each other with joy and laughter, until Nilima's mother called to go home.

Their love affair flourished for two years, meeting in the forest, talking endlessly until sunset. Words flowed easily between them, as if they had known each other forever. Religion, family, caste—none of it mattered in that moment. Laughter became their bridge, curiosity for their tether, and soon, friendship blossomed into something deeper. In the quiet moments, away from the crowd, they shared secrets and dreams, finding in each other a rare honesty.

One evening, as they met at their usual place under the sky full of stars in the dark, Nilima whispered, "Love doesn't belong to religion, to caste, to family. Love… just is."

But reality intruded. Nilima shared with Ravi that her parents are taking this very hard, and they told her, "A Muslim girl cannot marry outside her faith," they said. "You will obey us. We are arranging your marriage." Preparations began swiftly, the arrangements formal, the future already written in stone.

He smiled, taking her hand. "Then we will meet in our own way. We can be together forever."

Ravi continued, "My family will accept you no matter what. The teachings from my father showed me to treat people equally, regardless of caste or religion." It was the proudest moment for Ravi.

Nilima and Ravi planned to meet at the forest and bring her to his house for marriage in one month.

That night, Ravi spoke to his parents with joy and eagerness to express his love for her. He knows how benevolent his parents were. He felt profound happiness.

But their reaction was venomous. "A Muslim is beneath even the Dalit," Ravi's father said about the lower caste. "You will abandon your Shankar, your inheritance, all honor, if you dare to be with her." They cursed Nilima by name, refusing any acceptance, any reconciliation, any future that included her.

Ravi argued, "But you always said all humans are the same, you invite each and every one in this town to celebrate the holiday, and I have learn to accept people as they are!"

The father said, "ENOUGH! That is completely different; any other caste or other religion is not to be married into; we are the Brahmins."

The father continued, "It ruins family blood."

Ravi didn't want to argue but was torn between love and family pride.

Within a few weeks, the whole small town was aware of Ravi and Nilima. The relationship between the two communities was getting bitter. One thing led to another, and there were riots between the two religious groups. Arguing and pointing fingers at each other for this unlawful union of Nilima and Ravi.

The entire small town was abuzz with whispers of Ravi and Nilima. What had begun as quiet curiosity soon turned into open disapproval. The fragile peace between the two communities started to fracture, like a thin sheet of glass under too much pressure. One rumor led to another, and before long, anger spilled into the streets.

Riots broke out between the two religious groups — neighbors who had once shared meals and festivals now stood on opposite sides, shouting, accusing, and breaking. Each side blamed the other for this unlawful and unthinkable union between Nilima and Ravi.

Some claimed it was all a plot — "Nilima's family planned this," one woman hissed, "They want Ravi's wealth, they want to convert him." Others fired back, "No, it's Ravi's family! They're using their influence to turn us against each other!"

In the middle of all the chaos, love became the easiest target.

What began as something pure — untouched and sacred — was twisted into a symbol of betrayal, rebellion, and sin.

To love had suddenly become an act of defiance.

Nilima stood at her window, listening to the distant shouts that once were songs of her town.

She wondered — how could the love of two hearts shake the walls of so many homes?

How could something so gentle be turned into a reason for hate?

Why does it matter to them?

Where did the kindness, the compassion, the very soul that makes us human?

Her thoughts spiraled like smoke in the air.

To her, love had always been the purest of all truths — a force that sees beyond the color of skin, beyond the name of one's god, beyond the boundaries of class or caste.

But now, that belief trembled.

Because the world she had trusted revealed its stage — a grand theater of pretense.

Everyone was acting.

Her family, who lit diyas during puja and sent sweets across the lane to Ravi's home,

Ravi's family, who accepted them with smiles and blessings, was all a fragile performance of harmony.

Little did Nilima know that beneath those painted smiles, the roots of hatred ran deep, old as dust and stubborn as blood.

Society was nothing but a mirror hall of deception — each reflection showing what it wished to hide.

And yet, amid the noise and betrayal, Nilima's heart did not waver.

Against the storm, she held on to one truth — Ravi.

Her faith in him was not reasoned or measured; it was instinct, raw and absolute.

She trusted him with every beat of her heart, perhaps because she knew that without him, her life would no longer be hers to live.

Ravi walked the streets that once felt like home, but now every corner seemed to judge him.

The laughter of children playing, the gossiping neighbors, the prayers from the temples and mosques alike — all of it felt like a chorus of accusation, a constant reminder that he had become a target.

In his chest, love and duty were like twin storms.

Every memory of Nilima — the curve of her smile, the warmth of her hand in his — was a light he longed to follow. He remembers how her presence felt like life, like home. The few years of memories of her were his life, his everything. HE WANTS HER!

Yet the voices of his family, his community, and the town rang louder than his heart.

If I choose her, they said, everything will burn. Our homes, our honor, our name.

If I choose her, he thought, I will be the architect of chaos.

Ravi's heart ached.

He did not want to betray Nilima, yet he feared the cost of standing against the tide.

He saw the smoke rising from broken doors and shattered trust, and he felt the weight of centuries pressing on his shoulders.

This was not just love — this was a battle between the world he knew and the heart he desired.

He wanted to scream that love should not hurt anyone else, that love should not be a crime.

But the town was a jury he could not sway.

The streets whispered threats, the houses echoed anger, and even the wind seemed to carry disapproval.

And so, in the quiet of his room, with Nilima's laughter still ringing in his mind, he made a choice —

a choice not of desire, not of heart, but of fear, of duty, of a society that demanded obedience over truth.

He turned away from love, not because he lacked it, but because the world around him left no space for it.

Ravi closed his eyes, wishing he could rewrite the stars.

But the stars above were silent, indifferent, watching the young hearts of the town bend and break beneath human judgment. After days of unrest, smoke still hung over the town — and in that haze, Ravi made his choice. Torn between the woman he loved and the weight of his community's expectations, he bowed to the pressure.

After all this unrest...

Ravi reluctantly chose his social injustice over love.

Florida September 2021

Flux

Nilima woke up drenched in sweat, sitting upright on her sofa. Last time she was driving from work. Her consciousness is playing games with her mind. She didn't know if the short-term memories and long-term memories were even real. How did she go from driving to suddenly sitting on the sofa, with no memory of the time in between? How had she ended up here from her car? The vision she had experienced a few months ago was unlike any other, untethered from time, unbound by space. None of it made sense. She had not been alive in the 1910s and yet the memories—the sensations, the smells, the heartbreak—were seared into her mind.

She thought the religious struggle, the social injustice, and the discrimination against women hadn't changed despite the advancement of science and technology. People to this date behave the same!! That seemed to be the only truth she learned.

Regarding remembering an unrelated time and space, she craved the truth. She researched more into reincarnation. It was rather impossible to believe in the reincarnation of human lives, which doesn't add up mathematically or logically. So, she looked for answers once more…

The scientists called it cryptomnesia—forgotten fragments resurfacing in distorted form. But Nilima was not convinced. She came across Ian Stevenson's research: The cases of children in India who spoke fluent dialects they had never heard, and some who recognized relatives from a life they should not have known.

Ian Stevenson, a Canadian-born psychiatrist and researcher at the University of Virginia, devoted more than four decades to studying what he called "Cases of the Reincarnation Type." His work, which spans multiple cultures and continents, documents over 2,500 accounts of young children who claimed to remember past lives with striking clarity. These children often spoke of names, places, and events beyond their experience, sometimes even describing the manner of death in a previous existence.

Stevenson meticulously investigated these claims by interviewing families, cross-checking details, and recording physical evidence such as birthmarks or congenital deformities that eerily corresponded to the wounds or injuries of the deceased individuals the children claimed to have been.

His multi-volume series, Cases of the Reincarnation Type, offered not only anecdotes but rigorous case studies—methodically gathered testimonies, psychological evaluations, and cultural analyses.

Though controversial, his work remains among the most comprehensive attempts to bridge science and the possibility of reincarnation, leaving open the unsettling question of whether memory might extend beyond the boundaries of a single lifetime. Could these fleeting sensations be her own thread leading back to something older than childhood? Then she thought of the actual time…why are the 1900s so important?

Whispers From A Distant Shore

"Those who cannot remember the past are condemned to repeat it." George Santayana (1905)

Nilima was alone in the apartment, sipping on chai as she looked outside at the sunset and pondered about everything, she revealed…

Perhaps these are not just experiences or visions, but fragments of another consciousness — someone who once lived in the early 1900s. But why her? What are these visions trying to tell her?

She finds herself drawn to the lives of people who once walked the Bengal plains under British rule, yet she cannot explain why their shadows feel so familiar. How could the consciousness of another person, someone long gone, be echoing inside her mind?

Nilima has never been one to believe without evidence. She needs definitions, explanations, something tangible. And yet, this presence feels undeniable — intimate, insistent.

Why does the girl in her visions bear her own name? That girl from 1910 is not her. She repeats this to herself, almost like a prayer. But each time, the certainty wavers, just slightly.

Nilima knows little about Bengal under British law — about how people lived, suffered, or resisted. Maybe these visions are not coincidences at all, but a call to look deeper — into history, into herself, and into the unseen thread that connects one consciousness to another.

Because Nilima left Bengal for the United States when she was only twelve, much of her homeland's history was lost to her. The American school system taught her about wars she never felt and revolutions that were not her own, but not about the soil her ancestors walked on. Honestly, she never cared about her past or her ancestral history. She grew up with fragments — names without context, stories without endings.

Now, as these strange visions emerge, she feels history pressing against her — urgent, alive, almost pleading. Perhaps it is not just memory she is uncovering, but a consciousness that refuses to be forgotten. A soul seeking remembrance through her.

It was raining outside. Nilima sat by her window that evening. It was a full moon cycle, but the clouds covered it completely, making the evening darker than intended. She spends hours looking up Bengal under British rule, yet the more she reads, the more the words dissolve into something personal — as if she were remembering, not learning. Each piece of history is a piece of hers.

Nilima knew that before the British saw the Bengal region as a land of opportunity — rich in textiles, fertile fields, and endless trade — its people lived in quiet simplicity. The Bengalis were not driven by greed or restless ambition; their lives flowed with the rhythm of the rivers that nourished them. Their minds were not yet fractured by ideology or burdened by the ego-centric pursuit of self.

For centuries, they shared the same waters, the same monsoon songs, and the same storms that bound them together. Hindus and Muslims lived side by side — their festivals intertwined, their languages interwoven, their sorrows indistinguishable. I heard it from Dadabhai and Nanubhai (grandfathers) a few times, but I never cared.

As she continued her research, in the early 1900s, Bengal was both the jewel and the wound of British India — radiant with art and intellect, yet bleeding under the weight of colonial exploitation. From Calcutta, the imperial capital until 1911, the British ruled with rigid precision. Laws were written in English, judgments favored those in Western suits, and land taxes pressed heavily on the peasantry.

The Permanent Settlement Act of 1793 had already twisted the roots of Bengal's society. By granting land ownership to the zamindars (landlords) and reducing peasants to mere tenants, it transformed age-old agrarian harmony into a machinery of profit.

History unfolded under the shadow of colonial mentality — Bengal's children starved as the gap between the rich and the poor widened, while Britain grew wealthier from their suffering.

This is where Nilima paused and wondered: why do all the fingers point only at the British? In our grief, had we, as Bengalis, forgotten our neighbors — and the very philosophy that once bound us together? The division was not of land alone, but of memory, of faith, of belonging. In turning away from one another, we became strangers to our own essence.

She continued reading…

The Partition of Bengal in 1905, orchestrated by Lord Curzon, sliced through this harmony. It split the province into two: Eastern Bengal and Assam, where Muslims formed the majority, and Western Bengal, which belonged predominantly to Hindus. Curzon claimed the partition was for administrative efficiency, but the intent was far more cunning — to fracture Bengal's unity and weaken its growing nationalist movement.

A subtle line, invisible yet sharp, began to cut through the heart of Bengal. The Bengals' sentiments towards differences among people have kept us divided and unaware of our own karmic doing. The sentiments that should have bound us—language, heritage, longing—were transformed into quiet resentments, each nourished by pride and wounded history. Perhaps it was our own karmic doing, the unfolding of choices made in ignorance, the price of forgetting the truth that all separations begin first within the heart.

Nilima remembers her father speaking with quiet pride about the Bengal Renaissance — a time when art, poetry, and intellect stirred a new awakening in the land. The spoke of the Swadeshi Movement, of how people rose in defiance, spinning their own threads, writing their own stories, reclaiming the dignity that centuries of subjugation had eroded.

To Nilima, these movements were not merely historical moments; they were symbols of consciousness reawakening the people, remembering who they were. She agreed that they carried power, a collective stirring toward freedom. Yet beneath that noble fire, something darker persisted — an inherited fracture that never fully healed.

Even as Bengal rediscovered its voice, its people began to turn against one another. Division disguised itself as pride, and identity became a wound. The hate we carry for our own, Nilima thought, is not born in a day — it is down through generations, laced into the fabric of our collective being.

Now it has become the unnoticed norm—like walking through a vast fog. You catch a glimpse of someone from the opposite faith or status standing before you, yet you refuse to see them as human. We pass one another with quiet pride and silent hatred, still managing a faint, courteous smile. Within, the soul stands hollow—filled with ego, stripped of empathy. The true work lies not in the outer world, but within, where the self has yet to be awakened.

Freedom came, but not wholeness. Perhaps the true struggle is not against the colonizer outside, but the one that quietly survives within us — the colonial mind, the ego, the separation from our own essence.

As Nilima learns more about the period, a name surfaced, a surname, Sarkar. She remembers from the vision that was engraved on the library of Ravi's parents' house. She also remembers that the names on the portraits have the same surname, Sarkar. A Hindu upper caste that worked alongside the British agenda. She realized that the few Brahmin Indians were wealthy because of political ties with the British.

She traced the fading ink with her finger. Could Ravi Sarkar be the same figure who haunted her dreams or her past lover? The one whose voice seemed to call from another time. The one true love she ever felt.

Ravi's family had clearly benefited from the British presence, as seen in the Puja celebration. Did the rich Brahmin Bengalis' ties with the British cause discord among themselves? Nilima remembers her father used to say, "Some disguised themselves with the British, and destroy ties with their own people; that will not only have bad karmic return but bring agony for generations to come." Nilima never understood what that meant at the age of 12, or 16, or even at 21. Or that she didn't pay much attention to it.

This message bears within it a quiet truth — one of authenticity and humbleness, long forgotten amidst the noise of pride and possession. Perhaps this is what truly unfolded in Bengal: not merely a division imposed from outside, but one birthed from within — by a few whose greed sowed seeds of separation between caste and creed. What began as subtle distinctions hardened into the everyday rhythm of life, until the wound itself became invisible, accepted, and inherited.

Society, in its unawareness, moves like a herd — restless, unthinking, afraid to pause. The art of reflection, of stillness, of meditation on one's own thought, has faded like an ancient echo. Even now, generations carry the weight of old egos, measuring purity and worth through lineage and faith, binding love to boundaries that the soul never recognized.

As if our identity is not our character, but the labels!! Nilima was always tired of people labeling her about where she is from, the language she spoke, or what god she doesn't believe in. It is exhausting, and underneath it all, we are losing the very essence of being, what it means to be a human being.

The Nilima from the 1910s were the subject of violence. The idea of violence is not merely physical or something you can prove, but sometimes it is very subtle in nature. It can come as a neglect, it can be a strong thought without action, or even it's a duty to obey an unjust society.

Nilima imagined Ravi standing on his veranda in 1910 — watching and hearing the faint hum of protest, feeling something stir in his heart that he could not act upon. Perhaps that stirring was what reached her now, across time — a residue of his conscience that found refuge in her thoughts. Why did Ravi never think things through before getting into a relationship? Nilima realized Ravi is just like her, simple-hearted and under-observed about the surroundings!! Unaware that every action can be either a blessing or a disaster.

She realized that what she felt — this unplaceable ache — wasn't madness or imagination. It was heritage. The consciousness that spoke through her was Bengal's collective memory — a woven fabric of Hindus and Muslims, peasants and poets, oppressors and dreamers.

Every story was part of the same river, divided by history yet flowing toward the same sea. Perhaps feelings of Ravi also echoed with hers, duty and social acceptance have become the core of our beings…we are too scared to break the wall of division…

And as the night deepened, Nilima felt that river move within her — carrying voices that refused to be forgotten.

She falls asleep as she closes her laptop…

Deliverance

Suddenly, she glanced at the clock. 4:45 a.m. She hasn't slept much…

She rose, compelled by an unexplainable force. The beach called her. The crescent-shaped shoreline glimmered in the pale moonlight, like a silver smile stretched across the horizon. A single star hung vigil, unchanged, distant yet intimate.

At the gate, the familiar police officer greeted her, his voice gentle in the stillness.

"You sure like the beach at dawn!" he said with a knowing smile.

Nilima returned the smile, her eyes reflecting the moonlight on the waves. "Isn't it wonderful how the moon makes the water so… alive?"

He nodded toward the empty parking lot. "It sure does. Stay safe—hardly anyone's here at this hour."

She silently thanked him and stepped forward. The sand was cool beneath her feet, and the rhythmic clapping of waves drew her in. Only a few people were scattered along the shore, but they were distant, mere shadows in the silver dawn.

Today, she didn't want to sit. She walked, letting the warm water lap over her feet, feeling it rise to her ankles, her calves, then her waist. Her clothes clung heavily now, each step a slow, deliberate struggle against the ocean's pull.

The waves were gentle and forgiving, yet inexorable. She felt the water splash her face, the salt sting her skin, and a strange clarity settled over her. In an instant, she understood: her existence, fragile and fleeting, was about to dissolve, washed away like sand under the tide.

She looked up at the sky, and there was the crescent-shaped moon and the serendipity ever so bright---almost like sending a message to her. She couldn't look away.

And then, amidst the fear, a memory surfaced—a fragment she had written in her diary, a poem that had always given her courage. She recited it softly, letting each word anchor her to herself:

"Where the mind is without fear, and the head is held high

Where knowledge is free

Where the world has not been broken into fragments

By narrow domestic walls..."

As she spoke, visions exploded before her eyes. She saw her children—yet to be born, yet already part of her life—in a cascade of moments: infants, toddlers, teenagers. Every joy, every sorrow, every small triumph flashed in a single heartbeat. She was experiencing recent memories and short-term moments that were not on her radar, and then, something impossible happened…

British India 1910

She relived the life of Nilima in the 1910s again, the entire span from her birth to her tragic end at twenty. She saw Nilima standing up from the base of the tree and started to walk into the forest…dark, with the same crescent shape moon, and the star on the sky's horizon. Nilima kept walking until she came to a stop at the river shore.

It was astonishing — even now, she could hear Nilima's thoughts, raw and unguarded.

"I have nowhere to go. If I run away, I don't know where to go with the constant burden of betrayal and love, and if I go home, I will have to marry into a family forcefully. None of the options will set me free!"

The thought cut deep! Her freedom is stolen!

She felt betrayed, misled by the one person she trusted, the one person she unconditionally loved. She was also reciting the same poem of Tagore...

"Where the mind is without fear, and the head is held high

Where knowledge is free

Where the world has not been broken into fragments

By narrow domestic walls..."

Tears mingled with the night air as she felt the weight of her confinement, the suffocating grip of a world that did not belong to her. The only path she could see to true liberation, she believed, was the final one.

The young Nilima thought the only way to be set free was to die...with trembling hands, she unwrapped part of the saree and placed a large rock in it and anchored it on her waist.

The young Nilima thought the only way to set it free was to die, a choice that is independent of societal pressure, or pleasing the family, or accepting injustice. TO DIE IS TO LIVE FREE, she thought, as the Ganges River pulled her in. Without anyone noticing, the current of the river slowly consumed her as she took her last breath. She smiled, and she was happy...a choice without punishment, a choice without violence to others.

The river climbed her gradually, a gentle yet unstoppable force, as she sank beneath the surface. Pain, love, longing, and the desire for freedom surged through her in the icy current — every emotion, every memory, every stolen moment of happiness and hope, rushing past her like the river itself. And in that final moment, Nilima's spirit was both boundless and free, merging with the endless flow, leaving behind a world that had denied her the simplest gift: *choice.*

She stood there, unable to save her previous life. Unable to communicate or help her to see her worth…she was completely useless…

Florida 2021

As her vision disappeared, she was shaking. She turned toward the shore, fighting the invisible currents that tugged at her. Her legs felt shackled, as if anchored in the ocean, each step a monumental effort.

She has this profound desire to live, she thought, "*THE CHOICE TO LIVE IS MY DESTINY AND FREEDOM!! WHAT SHE COULD NOT, I CAN!*"

She shut her eyes, drawing in a long, shuddering breath that trembled through her chest and into her soul. She called on every fragment of strength she possessed — every sinew, every heartbeat, every spark of will — and pulled herself forward. The sand beneath her feet, coarse and unforgiving, became her ally. She staggered, faltered, almost succumbing, yet something deeper than survival — something primal, eternal— propelled her onward.

She sank to the beach, water retreating at her feet, and buried her face in her trembling hands. The cry that escaped her was unlike any other: a cry of joy, triumph, and liberation. Every grief, every longing, every thread of memory converged in that cry.

She was Nilima. She had always been Nilima. Nothing more. Nothing less. And for the first time, she truly knew herself.

The ocean stretched before her, infinite and forgiving. The crescent moon hung low, and the single star blinked, steady and unwavering. She breathed in the salt and wind, feeling the pulse of the world, and whispered to herself: the truth is me…here.

And in that whisper, she felt eternity itself — the river, the ocean, the sky, and the wind — all converging into a singular, radiant moment of clarity.

Nilima stood on the sand, the water retreating in gentle waves, and felt the weight of the world lift from her chest. Her survival was more than mere life; it was an act of becoming, a claim to her own being in a world that had tried to define her, confine her, and silence her.

She thought of life as a vast, boundless shore, stretching beyond sight, where every current of the river, every glimmer of a star, spoke in a language she was only beginning to understand. It was the language of a distant shore, one that whispered of freedom, of possibility, of self-unbound by expectation. Every step she had taken to reach this place, every breath drawn through fear and pain, had brought her closer to that language — a language written not in words but in choice, in courage, in the act of existing entirely.

The wind carried the scent of salt and earth, tangling in her hair like the threads of memory and longing. She realized that existence itself is indifferent — the river flows, the moon glows, and the stars blink — but in that indifference lies the ultimate gift: *the freedom to create meaning, to define oneself, to be whole simply by daring to live.* Like the moon tracing its slow, eternal path across the sky, she too could endure darkness and still shine, her own quiet luminescence on the distant shore of life.

Nilima whispered to herself, and to the river, and perhaps to the world that had tried to cage her: In that moment, she felt herself expand beyond the confines of body and fear. She was no longer just a girl who lost to expectation, no longer a story of grief or betrayal.

"I am here. I expand. I am me — and in my own consciousness."

Reference:

Encyclopædia Britannica. (n.d.). Temporoparietal junction. Retrieved August 28, 2025, from https://en.wikipedia.org/wiki/Temporoparietal_junction

ScienceDirect. (2021). Neuroscience of out-of-body experiences. Retrieved August 28, 2025, from https://www.sciencedirect.com/science/article/pii/S1550830721000951

WHRO. (2024, December 30). Since 1967, this small division at the University of Virginia has investigated the possibility of reincarnation. Retrieved August 28, 2025, from https://www.whro.org/education-news/2024-12-30/since-1967-this-small-division-at-the-university-of-virginia-has-investigated-the-possibility-of-reincarnation

Wikipedia. (n.d.). Ian Stevenson. Retrieved August 28, 2025, from https://en.wikipedia.org/wiki/Ian_Stevenson

Wikipedia. (n.d.). Jim B. Tucker. Retrieved August 28, 2025, from https://en.wikipedia.org/wiki/Jim_B._Tucker

Wikipedia. (n.d.). Satwant Pasricha. Retrieved August 28, 2025, from https://en.wikipedia.org/wiki/Satwant_Pasricha

ScienceDirect. (2020). Neural correlates of mystical experiences and spiritual states. Retrieved August 28, 2025, from https://www.sciencedirect.com/science/article/pii/S1053811919309944

Journal of Consciousness Studies. (2019). Reincarnation and the neuroscience of memory, 26(3–4), 45–62.

Pasricha, S., & Stevenson, I. (2017). Cases of children claiming past-life memories. Journal of the Society for Psychical Research, 81(2), 91–105.

Tucker, J. B. (2005). Life before life: A scientific investigation of children's memories of previous lives. St. Martin's Press.

Metcalf, Thomas R., and Barbara D. Metcalf. A Concise History of Modern India. Cambridge University Press, 2012.

Tagore, Rabindranath. Selected Essays and Letters (1905–1917), on Partition and Nationalism.

www.ingramcontent.com/pod-product-compliance
Lightning Source LLC
Chambersburg PA
CBHW040837010826
48978CB00012BB/794